══ CONTINUO ══

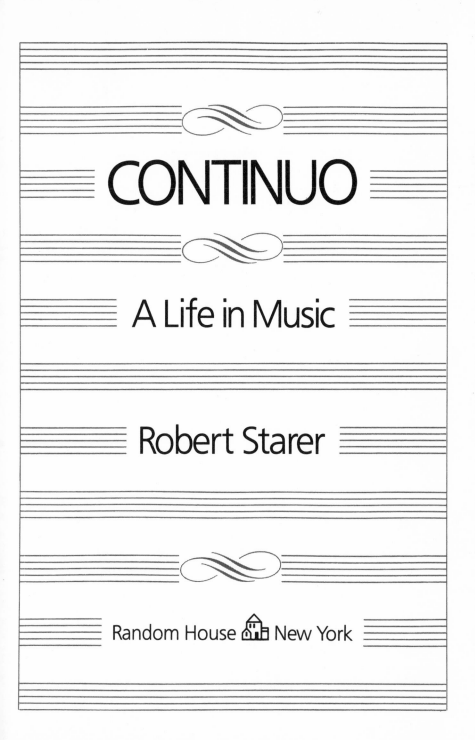

CONTINUO

A Life in Music

Robert Starer

Random House New York

Library of Congress Cataloging-in-Publication Data
Starer, Robert.
Continuo, a life in music.
1. Starer, Robert. 2. Composers—United States—
Biography. I. Title.
ML410.S81227A3 1987   780'.92'4 [B]   86-11897
ISBN 0-394-55515-5

Manufactured in the United States of America

Designed by Bernard Klein

To Gail

Continuo is the ever-present harmonic underpinning
in baroque music, performed and improvised upon by the
keyboard player.

R. S.

My thanks to H. Wiley Hitchcock and Robb Forman Dew for their encouragement.

Contents

List of Illustrations

≡ CONTINUO ≡

1. Pianos and Vienna

Victor Ebenstein taught piano at the State Academy for Music in Vienna. I studied with him from the fall of 1937, when I entered the academy at the age of thirteen, until the spring of 1938, when, soon after the German annexation of Austria, a man in a brown uniform came into the classroom and announced that all Jewish and half-Jewish students had been expelled from the academy and were to leave the building immediately.

Victor Ebenstein drummed his fingers on the desk and stared out the window when those of us affected by this edict got up quietly and left. Although his name may sound so, he was not Jewish. Names can be misleading; one of Hitler's ideological advisers, a man of supposedly Scandinavian origin, was named Rosenberg.

Some of my fellow students had happy smirks on their faces as they saw us walk out; others looked noncommittally straight ahead. Only my good friend Hans, who was the son of a Rittmeister (captain) in the old Austrian cavalry and liked to reconstruct historic battles with his tin soldiers—battles in which the Austrians were never defeated—got up, walked across the room to catch me at the door, grasped my hand and said, "I cannot tell you how sorry I am about this."

The German takeover of unresisting Austria must have been imminent all winter, but we young music students had paid little attention. My parents did discuss the threat to Austria's independence at the dinner table, but then they were always talking of imminent catastrophes. This one sounded no worse than some of the others; in any case, my fellow students' tales about their teachers' eccentricities were far more interesting. Many anecdotes were told of Emil von Sauer, the academy's most venerable teacher at that time. He was very old, and I was too young to know him. It was said that he often dozed during his lessons; yet no one gave a debut recital in Vienna without playing his program for von Sauer first.

Many teachers at the academy decorated their studios with photographs: of their younger and more famous selves leaning on pianos; of musicians of the preceding generation, with long, gushy dedications; and of their most successful students, with equally long inscriptions of exaggerated gratitude. When there was an interruption to the lesson, one's eye wandered up and down those long rows of photographs and one wondered, Did he really mean that? or I wish I had known him.

Victor Ebenstein's studio was quite bare; there were no photographs, memories or framed compliments. It held nothing but two grand pianos, and Ebenstein always sat at

one, ready to demonstrate something, play along with you
—very irritating—or invent little ornaments around some
passage you were repeating. Apparently he had never accepted the fact that he was teaching rather than playing
himself. Rumor had it that his promising career had been
cut short by some romantic tragedy. He spoke little about
himself, about the world or even about music. He asked few
questions, none personal, and tolerated no excuses whatever.
The girl who took her lesson just before me always left the
studio in tears. I never even knew her name; she was always
so distressed when she came out of her lesson that I couldn't
talk to her. What did he do to her to cause such suffering?

There was only one story Ebenstein told about himself:
The day he was to give his debut recital he had accidentally
cut off the top of his little finger. He played the recital
anyway, he told us repeatedly and always with the same
strange smile, although the keyboard was covered with
blood. How could you tell a man of such fortitude that you
could not practice because you had a cold?

I had begun to play the piano at an early age. Household
help was readily available in the Vienna of my childhood,
and I was raised by a varied assortment of provincial Austrian girls who had come to the capital to acquire domestic
skills and perhaps marry a soldier. Later, when my father's
textile factory had grown in size and importance, French-
speaking ladies of greater education were added to the
domestic staff. It was one of these, a thin, tall spinster who

liked to be called Gouvernante, who discovered that I had what is called absolute pitch, the ability to name the exact pitch of any sound heard. Actually this is not nearly as useful to the professional musician as many people assume, but it is the sort of thing an ambitious governess of a small child loves to show off to visitors. The guest would be asked to sing or whistle a note, I would identify it and then Gouvernante would go to the piano to prove that I had been correct.

When I was in elementary school, my high, sweet voice was also noticed. This, combined with the ability to always sing on pitch, made me a desirable candidate for the Vienna Choir Boys, a highly professional group that toured much of the year with its own traveling teachers. They did indeed want me, but my mother forbade it. She wanted me to have what she considered a normal childhood.

In those days my mother was studying psychoanalysis with Alfred Adler, and I saw as little of her as I did of my father, who came home late in the evening, always was elegantly dressed and never carried a package. This last detail impressed me a great deal as a child. My mother showed her love more openly; my more distant father took me on Sunday-morning walks, to which I looked forward all week. During these long walks, which we took alone, either in the Prater or the Vienna Woods, he imparted his philosophy of life to me. Whatever I can trace of my moral and behavioral values seems to have been implanted then.

Politeness, courtesy and consideration for others were considered marks of civilization. Even promptness was stressed; my father considered it proper to appear at an appointment exactly two minutes before the agreed-upon time. To be late was out of the question ("Punctuality is the politeness of princes"), and to be five minutes early showed too much anxiety.

Soon after dear Gouvernante had discovered my absolute pitch—she was much more proud of it than I—a proper piano teacher was engaged for me. He was a sour individual named Köppel. His weakness was that he liked political debate. When my mother was at home when he arrived—and she often made a point of being there—I tried to maneuver them into some topical discussion. This would shorten the time he could spend with me, since he had to leave promptly for his next lesson. In a few lucky instances they became so involved in their debate that they talked away the entire hour.

Herr Köppel firmly believed in repetition as the best way to improve. If I made the slightest mistake I had to play the entire piece again. This gave me little pleasure. What I really enjoyed was making things up at the piano. This was called *klimpern* (musical doodling) in Vienna and was strictly forbidden. Luckily for me my mother, in the next room, could not tell whether I was improvising—a word I did not know then—or practicing, and as long as sounds came from the piano she was satisfied. Often I put a book that interested me on the rack, read it while playing whatever came to mind and got away with it.

Even after I entered the academy—I was one of the youngest students admitted to that illustrious institute—I still preferred *klimpern* to mindless repetition, but of course I never told Ebenstein this. I can imagine his reaction; "criminal waste of time" would have been his mildest rebuke.

Victor Ebenstein was a disciple of the Leschetizky school of piano playing, and he believed strongly in the importance of strengthening the muscles of each finger. The ideal, which I heard mentioned often but never saw demonstrated, was to be able to put your hand on a glass-topped table and bring down each finger, even the fourth (the weakest by nature), with such force that it would shatter the glass. None of us had the courage to ask Ebenstein to demonstrate; besides, there were no glass tables in his studio.

Each lesson began with a half hour's worth of finger exercises, always executed in the same sequence, during which Ebenstein played whatever he liked on the other piano, often in a totally different meter and key. Since the two pianos were placed next to each other, he could occasionally glance over to see that one's fingers were raised high enough to come down with full force. I never thought that this discipline would lead to a brilliant pianistic career or was a "step toward Parnassus," but I must admit that even today, when I unexpectedly have to play the piano in

Robert Starer, age ten, at the gymnasium in Vienna

public, going through those exercises loosens the fingers quickly, no matter how stiff they have become from lack of use. The sequence in which the exercises have to be executed I will never forget.

In conversation with other piano students in the lounges and waiting rooms of the academy I discovered that other teachers believed with equal firmness in *their* systems as the only "true way of playing the keyboard." Some of them liked using the weight of the lower arm and therefore seated their students higher; others immobilized the upper arm completely by making their students hold a book under each armpit while playing; one went even further than Ebenstein and placed a coin on top of the student's hand; the coin had to remain in place while he played the piano. We students argued the merits of these diverse systems fiercely with one another. We also liked to trace back the line of our teachers' teachers, creating a pianistic genealogy similar to that of nobility. The further back you went, the more exalted it became. If your teacher had studied with Zemlinsky, for example, you could trace yourself through Liszt all the way back to Beethoven.

The Vienna of my childhood had many such historic tracings, particularly in music. What was called tradition was valued more highly than any creative endeavor. I do not remember ever hearing Arnold Schönberg's name at the academy, for example, although he had published some of his revolutionary ideas more than ten years earlier, and only once did a fellow student, a young man who did not do well at the academy and who must have had subversive leanings, ask me whether I knew Webern's music. I did not. Perhaps it is natural for a town with a glorious musical history to honor its past at the expense of the present. Every tourist visiting Vienna knows those little signs on inconspicuous-looking houses: "Here Schubert sketched his . . . ," "Here Beethoven contemplated . . ." or "Here Mozart sat with a cup of coffee." As the city grew shabbier over the years, it seems to me, those little signs became shinier.

The academy also had courses in music history and theory. Counterpoint was taught strictly and in the same fashion, we were often told, as it had been to Mozart and Beethoven. In those days Bruckner was considered at least on a par with Brahms, if not higher; Max Reger was usually linked in the same sentence with Richard Strauss; Sibelius was quite unknown and Mahler mentioned only rarely, except by my mother, who as a young girl had adored his conducting. Debussy and Ravel were not mentioned much either—but then, I am told, Brahms was not performed in Paris until well into our century.

In the Republic of Austria the state ran not only the academy but the opera house and certain concert halls as well. Thus, students at the academy had free access or very inexpensive tickets to a variety of musical events. Particularly desirable were passes to the opera, since, then as now, it was often sold out. For these student passes you had to arrive early—there was only a limited number of them for each performance—and the moment the gates opened you raced, two steps at a time, to the top gallery, where there was standing room for students. If you did well in that race of five flights, you stood in the center and saw the opera; if not, you ended up behind a post and saw very little. This added much to the excitement of going to the opera, and I made good use of my student pass. At only one other time in my life—my first year in New York, when I thought I would be there for only one season—did I attend as many concerts as during that winter before the Germans took over.

Going to concerts or the opera was not a new experience to me, but going without my parents was. My father had a great love of Italian opera and had taken me often during my childhood, but always to those comfortable, bourgeois seats that the student-standee of later years despised. The first opera I ever saw was *Aida,* and the visiting Dusolina Giannini sang her part in Italian to a local Radames, who sang his in German. I was perturbed by this and could not comprehend why these two were conversing with each other in different languages. I assumed, of course, that they were making the music up as they went along, just as I did at home.

My mother, who actually preferred the theater and often took my sister there, did like recitals and took me to hear —or as we now say, to see—Kreisler and Rachmaninoff.

It seemed to me then that an artist's success with his audience was measured by the number of encores he was asked to give. On this occasion Rachmaninoff had already given eleven, keeping me up long past my usual bedtime, when the audience began to stamp its feet and shout in rhythmic unison, "Prelude, Prelude." They did not stop until he played his famous Prelude in C-sharp Minor.

To get to the State Academy I had to take two different trams, slow-moving red streetcars like those still running in Vienna today, so slow that you could jump off and on between stops. My piano lesson with Ebenstein was in the late afternoon, and I was sometimes allowed to meet my father afterward at his *Stammcafé,* his regular coffeehouse. There the waiter would invariably greet me with: "Ah, hier kommt der junge Herr General-Direktor." Titles are very important in European countries. Many years later, during a year I spent in Rome, the maid at first called me Professore. When I dined without my jacket, I was reduced to Dottore; when she saw me without a necktie, I became Maestro; and after she had seen me in my undershirt I was only Signore. The waiter at my father's café was more imaginative and less precise in his use of titles.

My father often told me that the Vienna in which I grew up, the Republican Vienna of the twenties and thirties, was nothing compared with the "real" Vienna, the Imperial Vienna before World War I. Indeed, all those large baroque palaces, which had been the city homes of the nobility

My parents' wedding photo (1920)

during the winter season—they spent the rest of the year on their country estates in what are now Hungary, Czechoslovakia, Yugoslavia and Rumania—had already been turned into government offices and museums when I knew them.

We lived on the Gürtel then, literally the "Belt," a wide tree-lined avenue that encircled part of Vienna. From our windows I saw some of the violence that shook Vienna in 1934 when the "Reds"—the Socialists and their allies—battled the "Blacks"—the Catholics and Conservatives—in the streets and the army used artillery on the workers' quarters not far from us.

From our window I also watched the German troops enter Vienna in 1938. It was the first time in my life I had stayed up all night. In the late afternoon we had listened to Schuschnigg, the Austrian chancellor, make his sad farewell speech on the radio. He said that armed resistance was useless and ended, in a tear-choked voice, invoking God's mercy on poor Austria. Many people left Vienna that same night, some legally by train to friendly neighboring countries, others on foot through the mountains, where border control was less efficient.

My father understood the significance of what was happening. Although no one suspected what was really in store for many of us, my father considered leaving that night. As an exporter he had many business connections abroad. If my mother had not been in the hospital with a serious illness, I think we would have gone.

At first we heard the sound of many airplanes, far more than the Austrian Air Force had. The streets were quiet, almost deserted for a while. The Socialists and the Catholics, who had fought each other for possession of Vienna just a few years earlier, were now both enemies of the new rulers to come. They must have used those hours to find places of hiding, to escape or to think of how to live with the new regime.

Soon the first German motorized columns came down the Gürtel right under our windows—armored cars and those wide troop-carriers with helmeted soldiers displaying their ready rifles. Within seconds Austrian Nazis and other sympathizers appeared everywhere, carrying lit torches and shouting all the slogans rhythmically: "Sieg Heil" and— particularly significant in Austria—"Ein Volk, ein Reich, ein Führer" (One people, one country, one leader).

The next morning my father quietly opened a drawer I had never noticed before in his desk and removed his old Austrian army revolver. I went with him to a neighborhood park to bury it under a heap of trash. One of the first orders the Germans had issued was that no one was allowed to have arms, and my father apparently preferred burying his revolver to turning it in. Soon other orders followed, expelling Jewish students from institutes of higher education, forcing them to leave their secondary schools and go to one in the second district, the Leopoldstadt, where Jewish students were to have their own gymnasium.

In April Hitler made his triumphal entry into Vienna, and he too came right under our windows. There were two rows of German soldiers on each side of the street, and a policeman came to our apartment to keep watch with us, or rather over us. No window on the Gürtel was without a policeman. Hitler had returned to his native Austria, but he took no chances.

Was I frightened during those months of living under Nazi rule? Probably a few times. Physically I did not suffer. Only once, when leaving the building in which I took my Hebrew lessons, was I pursued and beaten by a bunch of thugs in brown uniforms. I lost a tooth that afternoon, but I got away and have probably never run so fast again. Being evicted from the academy and the gymnasium was harder to take, and certainly I understood that the world that I had been told would never see a war again because it had become "too civilized" did not exist. But I was not really frightened until the night in September when I left Vienna and realized that I was quite alone for the first time in my life and was going to a strange, unknown world at the age of fourteen.

In May 1938 Emil Hauser, formerly first violinist of the original Budapest String Quartet and then director of the Jerusalem Conservatory of Music, came to Vienna to audition young musicians. The British high commissioner for

Palestine had given Mr. Hauser discretion to offer a number of certificates of immigration to talented music students. I played for Mr. Hauser, was accepted and immediately began preparations to leave Vienna.

To get a German passport with a large *J* for *Jude* stamped on page one, you had to line up at the passport office the night before—another little humiliating harassment the new regime enjoyed imposing. When dealing with Nazi officials one considered oneself lucky to get to a German. He would be aloof and correct, whereas an Austrian might use his new power more viciously. Perhaps Austria, which had given its Jews freedom and equality in the nineteenth century, had allowed too many of them to reach prominence too quickly. The rest of the population must have resented that and now welcomed opportunities to put us down again.

Whatever the reasons, those of us standing or sitting outside the passport office all night—some two hundred people in all—did not really mind, since we knew we were about to leave. We were the lucky ones. My sister, who had belonged to a Zionist youth group, left even before I did to go to an agricultural school in Palestine and since then has spent her life in an Israeli kibbutz.

My father had booked a berth for me on an Italian ship that went from Venice to Haifa. To reach it I had to take the night train from Vienna's Südbahnhof, the South Station. My mother stood there, pale and speechless, in a black suit, a white blouse and a black hat. Also there was Kitty, a fourteen-year-old girl whom I had once kissed shyly. I had eyes only for Kitty, not for my mother, whom I was never to see again; she left for England with my father a few months later and died there during the war. I never saw Kitty again either, but only because six months later I no longer wanted to. My father was quiet that evening, a little solemn perhaps, but hopeful. He did come to Palestine at the end of the war, and though he did not recognize me when I met his ship in Haifa—it probably never occurred to him that the fellow in the blue Air Force uniform was his son—he adjusted quickly to life there and had some happy years.

What should I have said to my mother instead of staring at Kitty as the train slowly pulled out? At age fourteen the spirit of adventure is strong. When the Italian *bersaglieri* in their colorful uniforms entered the train at two in the morning (by this time I was quite used to staying up all night), the pale face of my mother had already faded slightly. I sensed that there was excitement ahead. When the train reached Venice and a barge took us to the waiting ship, I was even more convinced of it, and when I saw my first British soldier, complete with tropical helmet, her image disappeared altogether.

I did not see Vienna again until 1952, some fourteen years later. I had lived in Jerusalem for nine years, served in the

British Royal Air Force for three, had studied at the Juilliard School in New York City and was now teaching there. On a trip from New York to Israel I decided to stop off in Vienna to visit an uncle, the only member of my family who had returned. The factory that the Nazis had taken from him had been restored on condition that he live in Vienna and run it himself. He led an isolated life there; and while I was staying with him for a few days I looked at the town of my birth with adult eyes.

In 1952 Vienna was still under four-power occupation. The Russian soldier who checked my Israeli passport held it upside down as he stamped it with an illegible red mark. My uncle lived in the British sector, and with a foreign passport one could move around Vienna quite freely. When I went to the Russian sector once, to hear a lecture by Shostakovich, who happened to be in Vienna, I was immediately surrounded by inquisitive characters because I was wearing a nylon shirt, then clearly the mark of an American.

During those days I walked all over Vienna. The town had been severely damaged during the last year of the war, not only by air raids but also by artillery bombardments and street fighting. Very little had been restored. There were many ruins, and not even all the rubble had been removed. The house in which we had lived on the Gürtel was no longer there; the park in which I had played soccer as a boy held the remnants of a bombed-out factory; my father's old coffeehouse, his *Stammcafé*, was closed. I went to look for Hans, my dear friend, and learned that he had been killed at Stalingrad.

Finally I went up the steps of the State Academy for Music. The building was untouched, as was Victor Eben-stein's studio, which looked exactly the same. He seemed genuinely pleased to see me. Had he perhaps observed me carefully during all those hours when he seemed to be playing indiscriminate counterpoint to my finger exercises? Had he looked into my soul during those unloving sessions?

I did not ask him anything, not even how he had managed to survive the war, but for the first time since I had known him, he talked. He not only talked, he opened the drawer of his desk and brought out scrapbooks with reviews, and photographs of famous musicians who had approved of him and of students who had succeeded—all the memorabilia the other teachers had hung upon their walls. There was even a photograph of the young Victor Ebenstein, rather handsome, perhaps taken just before he had cut his finger on the day of his debut recital. I did not quite understand why he was suddenly showing me all this, but soon it became clear that he no longer loved Vienna, that he wanted to leave. In fact he was asking me to help him emigrate to America. It was sad to see this forceful man plead. He had been to America before I was born and asked after people whose names I did not know. He thought there was much he could give young American music students.

Ebenstein handed me a batch of papers and asked me to give them to the dean of Juilliard, which I did upon my return. The dean listened sympathetically, the way deans do, but I heard no more of the matter. Perhaps Ebenstein was considered too old to handle such a change of environment effectively. When I was next in Vienna, during the winter of 1957–58, he was no longer listed on the roster of teachers at the State Academy.

I have since been back to Vienna twice, both times with women who wanted to know the town I had grown up in —in 1957–58 with Johanna, a fellow student whom I had married in Jerusalem; and in 1975 with Gail Godwin, whom I had met at Yaddo, the artists' colony in Saratoga Springs, in 1972.

Vienna looked better in 1957 than it had five years earlier; it had begun to restore itself. Austria had regained its independence and the four occupying powers had left. The dollar bought much, and even with my meager fellowship I could rent an apartment for my wife and son, and a studio for myself. The studio had a seven-foot Bösendorfer piano and an old-fashioned *Kachelofen,* a coal stove, which had to be filled and lit every morning and then took almost two hours to warm the place, by which time I was often through with my work for the day. After a few days I discarded the heating ceremony and instead went to the café across the street to have a coffee "with" (which meant with schnapps, not milk), and then wore gloves while pacing up and down the studio. I wrote my Concerto for Viola, Strings and Percussion that winter, and when Howard Shanet, program annotator for the New York Philharmonic, which played the work the following season under Leonard Bernstein's direction, heard about this, he began his program notes with the following sentence: "This work was written literally with gloves on." Luckily I had not told him about the schnapps.

The concert halls of Vienna were half empty that winter, and there were no hordes of students rushing upstairs for the top balcony. When I asked the composer Gottfried von Einem about this, he answered, "We miss half a million Jews." Vienna seemed sleepy to me; there was no turbulence, only a desire to forget and be comfortable again. The country had begun to transform itself into a second Switzerland, politically neutral and safe, a country in which public transportation ran on schedule, the telephone worked and men with large brooms walked behind each garbage truck so as not to leave a single bit of refuse on the street. Some Austrians I talked to claimed that this was true only of the inner city, which the tourists saw, and that the rest of the country still lived in *Schlamperei,* a form of benign disorder more typical of the earlier Austria.

This "Swissification" of Austria was even more noticeable during my visit with Gail in 1975. This time I was truly a visitor, if not a tourist, in the town in which I had been born. We stayed in a hotel—the kind foreigners don't know about, but still a hotel—and I spoke German only when necessary. I discovered that I could no longer pass for a native; I had apparently lost my Viennese accent and couldn't retrieve it. Waiters thought I was a German pretending to know local slang.

Being a tourist in my hometown gave me an opportunity I had not had on earlier visits: to go to the *Heurigen,* the places where the new wine is drunk, in Grinzing and other Viennese suburbs. I had often heard my parents speak about the *Heurigen,* always with the giggles reserved for the drunken escapades of loved ones, but I had never gone to one on previous visits. Johanna did not drink any alcohol, and one does not go to the *Heurigen* alone.

Here I was at last in Grinzing, with the woman I loved, drinking that pleasant wine which has to be drunk while it is young. Gail liked it, and we nibbled at some of the infinite variety of sausages the Viennese concoct, talked to some other couples and listened to the symmetrical phrases produced by three musicians, who wandered among us. Each four-bar phrase they played made you imagine what the next four bars would be like, and invariably they were just as expected. I tried to speak to the most human-looking musician, but he rebuffed my attempts. Perhaps the only way for him to endure was to play his music and ignore his drunken audience.

As I sat in Grinzing sipping wine, many images came to

mind. I saw my parents, both long dead, sitting at a table in high spirits, loving each other as they must have when they were young; I tried to imagine what my life would have been like if the man in the brown uniform had not come to the academy that day in 1938; and I wondered whether Victor Ebenstein had been here during the war, perhaps wearing a small swastika in his lapel and drumming his fingers on the hard wood of the table to keep them in practice.

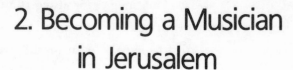

2. Becoming a Musician
in Jerusalem

I N 1977 the New York City Opera gave the American premiere of *Ashmedai,* an opera by the Israeli composer Joseph Tal. Tal was my first real teacher, certainly something of a mentor and at times almost like a father to me when I arrived in Jerusalem in 1938. He took a deep interest in me and guided me intellectually and musically through the decisive, formative years from fourteen to seventeen, when habits, tastes and views of the world are formed. He introduced me to the music of our century and, most important of all, gave me the courage to believe that my improvisations were not a childish waste of time but could lead to composition if they were disciplined and shaped.

As I went backstage after the premiere of Tal's opera at Lincoln Center and waited in line to shake his hand, much of what I owed him flashed through my mind. He is a small, slim, energetic man with clear but not cold blue eyes and a forehead that has grown higher over the years. He greeted me warmly, though we had not been in intimate contact since those early years and though I had left him for reasons that seemed compelling at the time but don't now. The people behind me in the line were pushing impatiently, and there was no chance to offer more than brief comments about his opera and the performance.

Since I was only fourteen years old and quite alone when I arrived in Jerusalem in 1938, the administrative head of the conservatory, a thin-lipped lawyer, became my legal guardian. Without asking me about my early upbringing, he assumed that his own way of life would fit mine. He boarded me with an Orthodox family and sent me to an equally Orthodox gymnasium (Palestine followed the European educational system).

The family I stayed with blessed the Lord before each meal and thanked Him lengthily after it but did not give me enough to eat. Sometimes at night the Yemenite maid sneaked food into my room. Although the demands of religious observance were rigidly obeyed, members of the family often behaved unethically and hypocritically, as I gathered from dinner-table conversations and other observations. They also let me know in many unsubtle ways that I depended upon their "loving kindness."

At the gymnasium, to which I went every morning from their house, Talmud was taught along with Bible studies and interpretation, and the students were divided during the lunch break into those who had brought meat sandwiches and those who had "milk." Perhaps if my legal guardian had put me up with a more sympathetic family and had sent me to a more liberal gymnasium, the transition would have been easier for me. As it was, I soon became restless and eventually rebellious. A way of life that attached so much importance to petty extensions of originally hygienic biblical law seemed pointless to me, especially at a time of approaching disaster, and I often had visions of buying a ham sandwich at one of the shops where British civil servants bought their food, and then asking the school principal in which section I should sit.

My parents' house had been Zionist but not Orthodox. I knew enough modern Hebrew to get along in most classes and quickly learned the new words used in science and math. But the study of religious subject matter, particularly the many different interpretations of a single biblical passage and the lengthy discussions and arguments about them, bored me. It was not until I was in my thirties that I saw the poetic beauty of Isaiah or Ecclesiastes and read them with real pleasure.

My father had given me three blank pieces of paper with his notarized signature at the bottom. "You might need these one day," he had said when he handed them to me just before I left Vienna. I now felt a little like the boy in the fairy tale who knew that three of his wishes would be granted. Even my legal guardian was powerless against these magic pieces of paper, and I used the first one to get out of that school. As for my Orthodox family, I simply ran away.

I moved through many quarters in the next two years,

living in rooms or apartments shared with other students or
in furnished rooms with a family, with or without board.
In some I stayed only a month, for not one of them was
pleasing or even satisfactory. The only fixed point in my life
was Joseph Tal and his house. He taught his theory classes
at the conservatory but gave his private lessons at home. I
saw him much more often than the one piano lesson a week
the conservatory had assigned us. Occasionally his wife
asked me to stay for a meal, which then stretched into a
whole evening of music and talk. Tal—his name actually
was Grüntal then; he dropped the *Grün* after the establishment of the State of Israel—lived in a spacious old Arab
house in the center of town. He had brought his piano,
books and music from Berlin, but the rest of the furnishings
were Near Eastern: mats on the floor, strings of beads rather
than doors separating rooms and a number of instruments
—ouds, reed flutes and drums—hanging on the walls.

Tal had studied with Hindemith in Berlin and knew the
music of Bartók, Schönberg, Berg and Stravinsky well. He
was actively involved in the music life of Jerusalem as
pianist, conductor, composer and teacher. When he played
chamber music with a group of string players or woodwinds, I turned pages for him; when he took a chamber
orchestra on a tour of the kibbutzim, I played the continuo
part in the baroque pieces on a one-manual harpsichord he
owned; when he rehearsed excerpts from an opera with
student singers, I went to all the rehearsals; and when some-

thing of his was performed in public, I was there as a matter of course.

His class lectures included aesthetics and a bit of philosophy. His thinking had been influenced by the German musicologist Hans Mersmann, whose theories have never caught on in the United States the way Heinrich Schenker's have. Tal insisted that his students know musical literature, and since none of us had record players or recordings, we went to public concerts of recorded music. There was a kindly old doctor with a lisp who played all the Beethoven string quartets for us, three every Saturday afternoon, and there was a bookstore owner who liked contemporary music, at whose store I heard *Le Sacre* for the first time. While we students made fun of the dear doctor's lispy pronunciation of "Budapesht Shtring Quartet," we were grateful to him for those Saturday afternoons. His wife served us lemonade and a cookie during the intermission that always followed the second quartet. The score of a Beethoven quartet cost as much as a lunch; by skipping lunch seventeen times in one winter, I acquired all of them. I still have them, torn as they are.

In Joseph Tal's theory classes one of my fellow students was a young soprano from Germany named Johanna. We soon went to recorded concerts together, I accompanied her at the piano and we often had—or skipped—lunch together. In 1942, when the Germans under Rommel were in

El Alamein—not far from us—and the British had evacu-
ated their families to India, we got married.

It was in my private lessons with Tal that the decisive
change from piano playing to composition took place. Even
in 1938, when these lessons began—and they were purely
piano lessons then—Tal concentrated more on musical content, understanding and interpretation than on manual dex-
terity. Once when he was out of the room briefly during
a lesson, I doodled a little without being aware of it. "What
was that you just played?" he asked when he came back.

"Oh, nothing," I said, "nothing."

"Play it again," he insisted.

"I couldn't. I really don't remember what I played."

"Next time you do that when you are alone, write it
down and bring it to me."

This was the first encouragement of my improvising I
had ever received. I went wild and at our next lesson
brought him reams of paper. He asked me to keep what I
considered worthwhile and to shape it better, more clearly
and without anything unnecessary. Thus the focus of our
lessons shifted gradually from what I was playing to what
I had written.

There are different attitudes about improvisation. Some
composers view it as an activity totally separate from composition; others improvise in the evening and compose the
following morning, thus letting the mind be its own censor

overnight; still others improvise until something worth noting down appears, then rush for the pencil before it is forgotten. Composers' views also vary on the topic of sketches: should they be kept or not? We know that Prokofiev kept his and sometimes used an idea several years later. On the other hand, Darius Milhaud told me when I was a student in Tanglewood in 1948 that if you cannot use an idea immediately, you should throw it away. "If you don't have another idea soon," he said, "you're not a composer anyway."

Tal considered improvisation a way to loosen the muscles of the musical mind. He suggested I write down only those ideas that deserved to be retained and had a memorable quality, not every rumbling of my musical intestines, and then work hard to give that idea the best possible shape before trying to develop it. There was no doubt in my mind that this was what I wanted to do more than anything else in my life, and before long I had completed my first feverishly "modern" composition and dedicated it to him.

Some years later, after I had written a trio for woodwinds, Tal arranged to have it played at a small concert of chamber music. To our surprise, Max Brod, friend and biographer of Kafka, came to the concert and wrote a glowing review for his newspaper, saying "Here is a young composer who writes from the depth of his soul." I no longer have the music, but I kept the review.

Tal was also concerned about my eventually making a

living in music by becoming a professional. The question
was pressing, since my initial scholarship was for only two
years and I would have to support myself at the age of
sixteen. He also thought in longer terms. "You will not be
able to live on your income from composing," he pointed
out, "not with the kind of music you like to write." This
prediction turned out to be correct. "You won't make your
living as a concert pianist either," he continued; "you get
bored too quickly playing the same music again and again."
Another correct assessment. "Perhaps you should learn an
orchestral instrument."

We looked into this, but decided that at fourteen I was
too old to take up the violin or the cello. We considered
various wind and brass instruments, but they had to be ruled
out because my teeth were bad. This left only the harp and
percussion.

The British ran a very active radio station in Jerusalem.
Some of the programs were in Arabic, some in English and
some in Hebrew. There was chamber music and solo recitals,
and there was an orchestra, which gave weekly public concerts at the Y.M.C.A. The orchestra had only one properly
trained percussionist, and when the music demanded additional players the conductor, a friend of Tal's, came to the
conservatory to recruit them. Thus I made my professional
debut—by which I mean my first public appearance before
a paying audience—as the fourth percussionist of the Jerusalem radio orchestra in a performance of Ravel's "Bolero."

I sat patiently behind a large suspended cymbal during the entire "Bolero" and bashed it vigorously six times near the noisy end of that piece. I received twenty-five piasters— there were a hundred piasters to the English pound—for doing so, and for attending four rehearsals. A few weeks later, after I played the triangle in the scherzo of Brahms's Fourth Symphony, I knew that this was not how I wanted to spend the rest of my working life. Tal agreed.

Now only the harp was left. The Palestine Orchestra, founded two years earlier by Bronislav Huberman and conducted in its opening concert by Toscanini, was located in Tel Aviv. It had brought a lovely lady from Hungary as its harpist, but the Jerusalem radio orchestra had no harpist. I saw a chance for a livelihood and began going to Tel Aviv once a week for a harp lesson with the Hungarian lady. Arab terrorism was at its height then, and each intercity bus carried a British soldier armed with a tommy gun. The soldier stood on the steps of the bus and kept the gun visible as the bus raced through Arab towns along the road. This only added to the excitement of my weekly trips, and my teacher often rewarded me with a sandwich or a piece of cake after our lesson. To her, playing the harp was the essence of life, and she insisted that I adopt the proper position for both hands and acquire the right finger technique. I did not seek such perfection, and as soon as I had acquired the rudiments of playing the instrument I was taken into the radio orchestra.

If the harpist looks alert and comes in at the right moment, very few conductors know whether he has actually
played all the notes or not. The harp does not often get a
solo and is used by some composers simply to thicken the
texture at moments of great intensity. Some years later,
while I was stationed in Cairo during my military service,
the Palestine Orchestra came to play in Egypt, and its
harpist, my former teacher, was ill. Since I was the only
known harp player in the area, I was asked to substitute for
her. There was only one piece on the program that called
for harp, *Concerto Gregoriano* by Ottorino Respighi, a piece
I had never heard or seen, and, as is normal in such a
situation, there was no time for a rehearsal.

I sat behind my teacher's harp, glanced at the most intri-
cate harp part I had ever encountered, and looked with a
heavily beating heart at the conductor, Bernadino Molinari,
a fine, experienced maestro. He must have sensed how I felt,
for he gave me every single cue and somehow helped me
to get through the first movement without any noticeable
mishap. When I turned the page to the second movement,
I saw 152 bars rest, then a single note repeated three times,
and then *tacet al fine*—nothing till the end. This seemed a
good opportunity to give my heart a chance to return to
its normal pace, so I dozed peacefully. Suddenly I noticed
that it was becoming very quiet around me and that
Molinari's eyes were piercing me. I grabbed the harp, his
hand came down, I played my note, repeated it three times

and trembled at my narrow escape. Those inconspicuous-looking notes were not only a solo, but some sort of dramatic turning point in the piece.

Later that year the British decided to entertain Allied troops stationed in Cairo—there were close to a million of them—by staging *The Merry Widow* at the Cairo Opera House, for the opening of which Verdi had been commissioned to write *Aida*. Again I was called on to play—an exposed but quite easy harp part. Luckily the harp does not play during the famous cancan and I watched the girls dance it every night, as did Egypt's King Farouk, who came often. I had one advantage: I could watch that bit of exposed thigh from the orchestra pit while he had to see it from his royal box. During *The Merry Widow*'s month-long run I also learned to admire the horn player who sat next to me. Every night during extended rests he went to the nearest bar, had a beer and returned just four bars before his next entry—without once looking at his watch. This kind of "professionalism" also convinced me that I did not want to spend the rest of my working life in the orchestra pit. Tal would surely have agreed, though by that time I was no longer his student.

Joseph Tal influenced me in one more major way by making me study Arabic music. He believed that someone living in Jerusalem should not train exclusively in the European tradition. He obtained a scholarship for me from an Ameri-

Playing the harp while in British uniform (Cairo, 1944)

can organization named MAILAMM, and I began to study
with Ezra Aharoni, a famous oud player, a Jew from Bagh-
dad. Since Aharoni did not know musical notation, our
lessons consisted of his playing something for me and my
writing it down and then playing it back to him. The oud
is not an easy instrument to master. The fingerboard is long;
hence quarter tones can be produced accurately. Quarter
tones are an essential part of Near Eastern music. The
trained ear distinguishes one scale from another by the
position of its quarter tones, and since each scale has a
symbolic significance, not recognizing a modulation from
one scale to another really means not following the music
intelligently. When I began to understand this, I realized
that systems other than our major-minor, modal, and
twelve-tone can have validity, and that music is by no
means a universal language. Learning to hear quarter tones
accurately took me some time. Only when I became famil-
iar with the many scales, the different rhythmic patterns and
their symbolic significance did I overcome the initial preju-
dice so many Westerners have that Arabic music "all sounds
the same."

Ezra Aharoni was a master teacher in an almost medieval
sense. He was surrounded by disciples—admiring students
who held doors open for him, offered chairs when he
wished to sit down and pulled them away when he chose
to get up. Occasionally he would honor us by playing
extended improvisations for us. Invariably he began slowly

Wearing an Arab headdress (Jerusalem, 1938)

and softly and remained in the same scale for quite a while, until he warmed up and the music quickened, changed scale more often and became more and more excited. It was as though he had to get into the proper mood to develop his musical ideas. His improvisations never began at a high point of intensity, as some Western music does.

After two years with Ezra Aharoni I had a sizable notebook full of oud music: scales, exercises and even some of my own. More important, I had written down a large number of his improvisations; he wanted to have them notated. When I left Jerusalem in 1947 to study in New York I could take only essential luggage. In my youthful ignorance I decided that my notebooks with Ezra's music were not essential. It is true that the musical world then showed almost no interest in what is now called ethnic music, but how I wish I had those books today. They would be invaluable, since he has long been dead and he was truly one of the greatest oud players.

Joseph Tal thought I should show my appreciation to MAILAMM, whose scholarship I had enjoyed for two years, by writing a composition for oud and orchestra. I did so, sent it to New York and forgot all about it. A few years ago the well-known oud player Mgrdichian called me in New York. Somehow he had heard about my piece for oud and orchestra, and since he was looking for repertory, he wanted to see it. My curiosity was also aroused. What sort of East-West synthesis had I attempted back then? To trace the manuscript was not easy, since MAILAMM no longer existed. Finally I located it in the Jewish collection of Lincoln Center's Library of the Performing Arts. I asked for my manuscript but was told that it was no longer mine; it had been donated to them and was therefore now theirs. However, they did make a photocopy for me. A quick glance at the manuscript convinced me that it should stay where it was, deeply buried in a library. I never even showed it to Mgrdichian.

When I was seventeen, a strange change occurred within me: I suddenly became critical of Tal. His music seemed too cerebral; his comments about mine missed the point; his opinions on almost everything were different from mine. At the same time I began to idolize another composer, Oedoen Partos. He was a brilliant viola player, first violist of the Palestine Orchestra and often soloist with it, as well as a fine composer. He was a tall, fair, impressive-looking man in spite of a limp, the cause of which I never knew. Partos had truly lived the convictions of his life. As a young man he had been a Communist and, instead of discussing ideology and politics in the coffeehouses of Budapest, had gone to Russia to live there under Communism. Disillusioned at about the time Arthur Koestler was, he had turned to Palestine, where he spent the rest of his life.

I had gone to all the concerts at which Partos appeared for some time before I mustered the courage to make an appointment with him to show him my music. He liked it and said he would gladly accept me as his student, but that this could not be done in secret and that to work with two teachers simultaneously would confuse me. This meant that I had to leave Tal. To tell him so was much more difficult than to end a love affair, and I don't think I handled it well. Yet I am not sure that I could do it better today. How does one leave a man to whom one owes so much? What reasons does one give and what justifications? What does one say that does not hurt? At the time I was so anxious to work with Partos that I surely caused my mentor unnecessary pain.

I did not see Tal for several years after our difficult parting. I served in the Air Force and went to Juilliard to complete my studies. When my first piano sonata was to be published in New York in 1950 I wrote him to ask whether I might dedicate the work to him. He replied in a brief note that he would accept the dedication. More recently, when a young woman who was "researching" my youth for a Ph.D. thesis on my piano music wrote to him, he answered kindly and at length. I have spoken to him on various occasions since, in Jerusalem, where I have visited many times, and in New York, but never again with the intensity or the depth of communication of those early years. We had gone in different directions musically, too. When electronic music first appeared we were both interested; he went into it wholeheartedly, whereas I discarded it after a few months' experimentation. He founded the first, and for many years the only, electronic music studio in Israel. His studio was eventually incorporated in the Hebrew University, and Tal became a professor there. Later he turned toward musical theater and wrote a number of operas, one of which, *Ash-medai,* was seen in New York.

During the summer of 1978 Tal and I appeared on a discussion panel at the World Congress for Jewish Music in Jerusalem, together with Milton Babbitt, Ralph Shapey and several Israeli composers. The question each of us was to address was: Is the music I write Jewish? Tal spoke briefly and said in essence that since he had lived most of his adult life in Israel, his music naturally was Jewish. For me the answer was not so simple. I had spent most of my adult life in the United States and considered only some of my music Jewish in nature. I tried to define it by saying that my Jewishness was sometimes in the foreground, sometimes in the background. I also said that I thought there were four components to be considered: heredity, upbringing, intent and language. We have no influence on heredity and little on our upbringing, though I did choose to learn Hebrew as a child. We do control our intent; such works of mine as *The Dybbuk* or *Samson Agonistes* were intended to be Jewish; *The People, Yes* and *Voices of Brooklyn* were not. Finally, language: when I follow Hebrew word rhythm I write different music than when I follow English word rhythm.

The meeting was followed by the usual reception, during which discussions continue and opinions that the speaker forgot or omitted while on the podium are expressed. Tal and I found ourselves alone in a corner, and I tried to formulate a generalization about how different his life and mine had been. He looked sternly at me and did not respond.

In each of us there are many components that we can draw upon or bring to the foreground when the situation requires it. When we face people who matter to us, we tend to stress those components they like to see, or that we *think* they might like to see. Sometimes a facet emerges that is quite beyond our control.

I can draw upon the European or the Semite in myself; the paternal or the filial; the professor or the knowledge-hungry student, and many more. But when I am in the same room with Joseph Tal, one uncontrollable facet emerges: I am still the adolescent who feels guilty for having left his benefactor.

3. An Arab Opera

IN pre–World War II Palestine there were two factions among the Arabs: those who were willing to tolerate the Jewish immigrants who had begun to arrive from Europe in increasingly large numbers, even to cooperate with them; and those who opposed them fiercely, even violently. Among the latter was the Grand Mufti of Jerusalem, who fled to Berlin when the war broke out and later helped organize the unsuccessful pro-Nazi revolt in Iraq.

And yet a member of one of the most powerful Arab families, one of the strongest opponents to Jewish immigration and settlement, found his way to the Palestine Conservatory, perhaps the only Arab who did. His head was full of music, he said, but he did not know how to write it down. He wanted help in notating his musical ideas so that others could perform them, and he would gladly pay for this service. Probably because of my interest in Arabic music and my experience in writing down Ezra Aharoni's improvisations, the head of the conservatory brought Akhmed and me together. The job seemed truly a gift from Allah; it paid much better than the miserable piano lessons I was giving, it promised musical interest and it might offer me a glimpse into a world not easy to enter. Akhmed found me acceptable in spite of my youth, and the head of the conservatory, interested in good relations with a member of a prominent Arab family, provided us with a room as a neutral meeting ground for the biweekly sessions between a young Jewish student from Vienna and a supporter of the Grand Mufti of Jerusalem.

Since the invention of the portable tape recorder the work of the ethnomusicologist has become relatively simple. The equipment can be hidden or disguised, the microphone is small, and so the proverbial old man or woman in the proverbially obscure village can sing unselfconsciously, often unaware that the singing is being recorded. The ethnomusicologist can then return home and transcribe the tape at leisure.

At the time of my biweekly meetings with Akhmed we had to follow a different procedure. Writing down music takes longer than singing it, so we had to take it a phrase at a time. Akhmed would sing a phrase for me: I would write it down as quickly as I could and ask him to repeat it, just to check. The second time he would sing it slightly differently, so I would sing both versions back to him and ask him which one he truly meant. He would then sing it one more time, in yet a third version. Later I read that Béla Bartók, in his travels through the Balkans to write down authentic folk music, encountered similar difficulties. At the time I was utterly puzzled by it, having been brought up with a Westerner's respect for accuracy and the written note.

Akhmed was composing a large-scale work, an opera, and a modus operandi had to be found quickly if it was ever to be completed. I evolved the habit of writing the notes down first in rhapsodic, expressive melodies and not worrying about rhythmic precision, since the rhythm tended to vary in his singing. In rhythmically repetitive tunes, on the other hand, no variation of basic meter occurred, but the pitches of the notes were somewhat different each time he sang. When we had several versions of the same melody, I sometimes sang them all back to him and asked him which he preferred. In a few cases I simply chose the one *I* liked best. This may not have been entirely ethical, but it did help us progress.

Once, after a particularly good session, Akhmed asked me to have a cup of coffee with him. He took me to a café the British frequented, and as we sat on low stools sipping Turkish coffee surrounded by pipe-smoking Englishmen, nargileh-smoking Arabs and a few cigarette-smoking Jews, he talked to me about his views on life. He was not as anti-Jewish as a member of his family might be expected to be, but he had only unkind things to say about women. He considered them impure creatures and really thought men were better off without them. I was sixteen then, and although this may seem inconceivable to a young man today,

I did not understand what he was hinting at. I simply disagreed with him and told him that I found women most desirable, utterly mysterious and quite unapproachable. Akhmed smiled, as though he knew better.

I mentioned this conversation to my friend Gideon, who was older and more experienced than I. Gideon was good-looking, with his thin nose and blond, straight hair, and spent all his afternoons at another café smoking cigarettes. Women found him attractive and he often bragged to me about his seductions and illicit meetings with married women, all related with flourishes and exciting details. Having seen me with Akhmed, he gently warned me that perfectly normal boys could go "that way" if introduced to that mode of life at my age. I listened, but I saw no danger; my musical sessions with Akhmed were proceeding well, and he never touched me.

Then one day Akhmed invited me to his house. This was a new turn, and I went to consult Gideon at his café. "I would like to go," I said. "I don't want to offend him, and besides I'm curious. One is not often invited to an Arab's home."

"You should go," Gideon said. "In fact, you *must* go. What you might do is take a girl along, perhaps Rina."

Rina was one of our fellow students, a cellist who was extremely feminine, buxom and blond. I had often looked at her from a distance, and she had been part of my nightly fantasies.

"Rina will never go with me. I don't think she knows
I exist."

"Let me speak to her," Gideon said.

To my surprise Rina agreed to go with me. It would be
the first time she and I were alone together, making it a
doubly difficult afternoon.

Akhmed's house was in the Moslem section of the old
walled city of Jerusalem. If you knew only the narrow,
winding streets of the crowded suks, the markets, as I did,
you would never suspect that such a spacious house could
be among them. All that could be seen from the street was
a heavy iron gate, closed from the inside, with a small hole
at eye level. We pulled a chain but heard nothing; the bell
must have rung inside the house. In a minute the eye hole
was opened, then closed again, and we were admitted by a
tall servant who led us along a path shaded by old trees to
the house. We were ushered into a large, elegantly furnished
room with comfortable chairs, where we waited for
Akhmed.

I had been told that according to Arab custom if the host
speaks with you for a while and then says, "I will now go
and make coffee for us," he is treating you as an honored
guest. If he asks his servant to make the coffee, he is honor-
ing you a shade less, and if he does so soon after your arrival,
he does not wish you to stay long.

Akhmed entered the room we were waiting in with a
warm welcoming smile, which disappeared when he saw

Rina. He bade us sit down—we had both risen to greet him —and almost immediately dispatched the servant to bring coffee. He and I exchanged a few polite words, Rina wisely said nothing and we soon left. It was probably not the most diplomatic way to deal with his invitation, but it did avoid trouble and clarified the situation between Akhmed and me. Gideon's advice had been good.

My musical meetings with Akhmed continued, but we no longer went to the café together after our sessions. We kept working until his entire opera was down on paper. I thought our meetings would end then, but Akhmed said, "And now I want you to orchestrate my opera; I want you to make it sound good, like . . . like the American movies." He must have had in mind Bernard Herrmann's or Max Steiner's scores, which employed a sensuous, rich, late-romantic orchestration. (This was long before film directors had discovered the eloquence of silence or evolved the technique of driving the sensitive listener to despair by repeating a single melody endlessly.)

I thought I knew what Akhmed wanted. Again the fee was generous, and I set to work in somewhat the same way I had orchestrated folk-song potpourris for the radio orchestra, only richer, as I had been instructed. A few weeks later I delivered a full score to Akhmed at the conservatory and recommended a copyist to extract the separate instrumental parts. While I could have used the money, I considered it beneath my dignity to do it myself.

The following spring I received an invitation and two tickets to the performance of Akhmed's opera. It was being given in a movie house in the Moslem section of Jerusalem, outside the old walled city, near the Damascus Gate. Jews and Arabs had agreed on a temporary truce to support the British war effort by then; even so, the mood was tense in Jerusalem and I did not relish the thought of being perhaps the only Jew at that performance. But my curiosity was strong—I did want to hear the result of all these months of work—and without consulting Gideon or anyone else I decided to go. Again I invited Rina to come with me, and again she accepted. She must have been almost as curious as I.

We got to the theater early and were greeted at the door by Akhmed. He smiled politely at Rina and turned us over to an usher, who led us to the first row of the balcony, which served as box seats. Soon the hall filled. There was a sprinkling of British civil servants, including the deputy high commissioner, who all came in black tie and sat together. There were Arabs in European suits and a few in galabias, their flowing white robes. The program was printed in Arabic and English, and I looked in vain for my name on it; I was not even listed as orchestrator.

I did not understand the reason for this slight until the music began. Akhmed had thrown my entire orchestration out the window, and the whole orchestra, from the highest flute to the lowest bass, played his melodies in imperfect unison. Musicologists call this heterophony, a noble term that really means a group of musicians trying to play together and not quite succeeding. This certainly describes that evening, but I was soon convinced that Akhmed's decision had been absolutely right. This way everyone heard his melodies clearly; adding Western harmonies and sounds would only have diminished them. Each song or aria had more verses than I had been aware of and the singers repeated Akhmed's melodies many times in that nasal way of singing that Arabs like, which is utterly different from our ideal of *bel canto,* the simplicity of Western folk song or the hoarseness aspired to by some rock singers.

Akhmed's melodies set his audience on fire, and even the British civil servants must have hummed them on their way home. Altogether the performance went well; when it was in any danger, a prompter, seated in full view at center stage, soon put matters right. The opera was a great success, and at the end Akhmed took many bows to enthusiastic applause.

After the performance there was a small reception in the downstairs lobby of the movie house. Akhmed's smile turned from triumphal to wistful when he saw me approach. As soon as he discovered that I was not the least bit angry because he had not used my orchestration, but on the contrary expressed genuine warmth for his achievement, he embraced me—the only time he ever did so—and we parted friends.

4. Hermann Jadlowker

THE Palestine Conservatory of Music, as it was called in the days of the British Mandate, occupied the second floor of a large old Arab house on Zion Square, where Ben Yehudah Street, coming from the new Jewish quarter, met Old Jaffa Road, which eventually led to Jaffa Gate and the Old City of Jerusalem. An Arab policeman, wearing the high, black fur hat the British had kept as part of his uniform from the days of the Ottoman Empire, walked up and down near the building, as did a highly made-up middle-aged Jewish woman who occasionally strolled away on the arm of a British soldier or an Arab in European dress to a small hotel just around the corner. When one of my fellow students once asked her why she walked this particular stretch, she answered, "That is my profession." After that we always referred to her as My Profession when we spoke of her. The policeman was often seen chatting with her. Our British rulers were not overly concerned with the morals of the populace.

Around the corner from the conservatory was the bookstore where weekly concerts of recorded music were given (to which music students were admitted for very little money). There were also some quasi-international grocery stores, where British civil servants could buy non-kosher food. The square itself, a noisy, smelly place, was filled with venders of falafel and tamarindi, a date drink. Not only cars and buses but mules, horses and even an occasional camel passed right under the conservatory's windows.

A broad staircase on the outside of the building led to the conservatory itself. One afternoon a well-dressed older man, tall, thin and with a proud bearing, walked up the steps and entered the office. The students who happened to be around that afternoon—I was among them—watched with fascination and curiosity; we could not imagine what a man with his looks, attire and manner could be doing in our school. As soon as he left we rushed into the office to question the secretary. Who was this man and what did he want?

We were told that his name was Hermann Jadlowker; that he had been a famous tenor in the early part of the century; that he had sung under the direction of Gustav Mahler and at the Metropolitan Opera House in New York; that he had participated in the world premiere of Richard Strauss's *Ariadne auf Naxos*; and that Kaiser Wilhelm had called him "my Lohengrin." Now he wanted to give concerts again and was looking for an accompanist—someone young and good at sight-reading who was willing to work. Previous experience was not necessary.

Hermann Jadlowker as Rodolfo at the Metropolitan Opera in
New York (1910) MUSIC DIVISION, NEW YORK PUBLIC LIBRARY

This was an exciting proposition and several young pianists showed up at the auditions a few days later. The head of the conservatory was present, as were several piano teachers and, of course, Hermann Jadlowker himself, who sat quietly through the proceeding and never let on what he thought. Afterward, all the pianists who had auditioned waited outside, and a few minutes later the head of the conservatory came out to announce that Jadlowker had chosen me.

At that time I was sixteen and living with three other music students, two from Germany and one from Czechoslovakia, in a two-room apartment just outside Jerusalem. Our landlord was a Jew from Kurdistan—an Oriental, as we called every non-European—who did not mind what we did as long as we paid our rent. Our constant practicing did not bother him, nor did the fact that our apartment was never cleaned. There was no refrigerator, and to keep the ants out of our food we stored it on a table each leg of which stood in a plate full of water. My elder sister, who was attending an agricultural school near Kfar Saba in order to become a useful member of a kibbutz, once came for a visit, but when she saw the place she quickly turned around and left.

What a contrast to the apartment where I had my first meeting with Hermann Jadlowker. It was his niece's apartment in Rehaviah, one of the nicest sections of modern Jerusalem. There was a Blüthner grand piano, which he must have brought with him from Germany, books in many languages and much music. It had a cultured, civilized atmosphere such as I had not encountered since leaving my parents' home in Vienna.

Jadlowker told me that we would meet twice a week at first, perhaps more often later, and that he would pay me five piasters per session. We began to work immediately. He put a volume of old Italian arias on the piano and held a second copy in his hand—he never looked over my shoulder—while we went through a number of them. He walked up and down the rather large room, usually simply "marking" the music, but occasionally singing in full voice.

Just to play that lovely Blüthner was a joy. My father had given me a small grand to take with me to Palestine, a dark-brown piano of undistinguished make. During my first two years there, when I changed my address almost every other month, that poor piano had been dragged from one place to another on a horse-drawn cart so many times that it was scratched on all sides and no longer could hold tuning. Melech Hasabalim—the King of Porters, as he was called—knew the instrument so well that whenever I went to the place where the porters hung out he greeted me with the enthusiasm reserved for good customers. He was a Jew from Iraq, incredibly strong, and proud that he could carry a grand piano alone on his back, secured only by a strap across his forehead. When we sat on his horse cart, the piano loaded behind us, on our way to my new lodgings, he would make conversation about "Hertel," as he pronounced Hitler, always adding "may his name be erased." Melech Hasabalim saw him as a reincarnation of the biblical Haman, who wanted to obliterate the Jews, and he was sure that there would soon arise a new Esther to thwart him. I listened to his notions in silence and never told him that I had once borrowed a swastika from my friend Hans and gone to see "Hertel" from as near as one was permitted to see him. Melech Hasabalim would not have understood such pointless curiosity.

So much for my poor piano; I sold it in 1947, before I went to America. Jadlowker's Blüthner responded to the slightest touch of the finger, to the slightest whim of the musical imagination. We went over much musical repertoire during the following weeks: Handel, whom he loved; a little Bach, whose vocal writing he considered unsuitable for himself; German lieder from Schubert to Mahler, with particular stress on Brahms; some arias from Italian and Russian opera (Jadlowker had been born in Riga and, as a Latvian, knew Russian); some Hebrew folk songs; and tidbits from here and there. Although he had been the kaiser's favorite Lohengrin, he would no longer sing Wagner.

My roommates were interested in my work with Jadlowker. When I told them that he wore a different suit at each rehearsal, that he always wore a necktie and that he tucked into his breast pocket a handkerchief that carefully matched his tie, they were incredulous, for it was so different from what we saw around us. Even Ben-Gurion, already then a man of great prominence, never wore a necktie, not even at the most formal occasions.

But our interest in Jadlowker's world went much deeper than mere apparel. What did he symbolize to us, four European teenagers separated from their parents and homes, transplanted into a world of Arabs, Jews from strange countries and Britons, and with little in common save our burning desire to make music our profession? His propriety, courtesy and orderliness represented our parents' world to us—at least I know it did to me. We envied him his experience, both musical and general, and his rich, successful life. We admired him for wishing to make a new start in surroundings he must have found as trying and different from the past as we did.

In some ways my friends and I were probably mature beyond our years and had learned to deal with unusual and unexpected situations; in other ways we were quite childish. Once when I came home from a rehearsal with Jadlowker, I found my friends feeding canned goose-liver pâté to our cat, whom I had named Schnurrli, an Austrian term of endearment derived from the German verb *schnurren* (to purr). Soon after the outbreak of World War II we had seen fit to stock up on food and had bought, of all things, ten cans of goose-liver pâté imported from France. That afternoon, the three of them had decided that the war was not going to touch us, and that Schnurrli, who was not feeling well, needed cheering up. The cat whined miserably and turned up his nose at the pâté. Soon after that he became so sick that we decided to take drastic measures. We had all heard that people who wanted to commit suicide took overdoses of sleeping pills, so we fed Schnurrli a large number of aspirins, hoping to put him out of his misery. He slept for seventy-two hours and woke feeling much better.

In spite of our youth we were all involved, though only peripherally, in the Haganah, the Jewish self-defense organization. We carried messages and occasionally small arms or ammunition to outposts, the sort of thing boys do well and get away with more easily than men. Arab terrorism, minor manifestations of which we encountered almost every day, was something one could respond to actively, quite unlike what was happening in Europe. Although news of the full extent of the horrors there had not yet reached us, we all knew how lucky we were to be out of it. By then my parents had gone to England, and the parents of most of my friends were safely in North and South America. I must have felt the need to respond more actively, for I was the only one of our group to volunteer for service with the British forces as soon as I reached the required age.

But the chief concern of our group was music; all our efforts were directed toward understanding it more deeply and performing it better. Eventually all four of us became professional musicians, though only one of us remained in

Jerusalem. Today one is first violist of the Orchestre de la Suisse Romande in Geneva and gave the European premiere of my Viola Concerto there in 1959; another is concertmaster of one of London's orchestras; and the third became host of a musical quiz program on the Jerusalem radio.

When Hermann Jadlowker first engaged me, he told me that it would be part of my job to correct him. I did not take this seriously. First of all, I did not believe that he would make mistakes; secondly, how could a mere music student correct a world-famous singer? The first time he made a mistake, I did not have the courage to speak up and quickly tried to change the accompaniment to fit what he was singing. He noticed, though, and stamped his foot in anger.

"Why did you not stop me? You are supposed to tell me when I make a mistake. That's what I am paying you for."

I understood then that he meant what he said, and that he did need me. He was going over old repertoire, music he might not have looked at in years—he had sung mostly nineteenth-century opera all his life—and when he made mistakes he preferred to be corrected by a young person rather than by some old vocal coach, or Korrepetitor, as such people were called. From that moment on I became more his collaborator than his accompanist.

The five piasters an hour Jadlowker gave me was good pay in my circumstances. With that you could buy fifty oranges or a bag of olives—the two cheapest food items—

at the fruit market. It was also considerably more than I got for giving piano lessons, most of them to unwilling children who had to be cajoled or coerced into playing and always seemed to live in the most distant corners of the city. At this time I had just lost my most promising student, a physician's sixteen-year-old daughter to whom I had been giving lessons in return for dinner, my best meal of the week. Her father fired me because he thought she was showing undue interest in me. In fact she wasn't, but the mere possibility must have seemed a threat to the doctor. In any event, it was a welcome change to work with Jadlowker in his niece's elegant apartment and to be paid for what seemed more like a privilege.

Our rehearsals always began on time. Jadlowker did not live at his niece's apartment, but he was always there when I arrived. Neither before the rehearsal nor after it was there any conversation not related to our work. He asked me no questions about my life and revealed little about his. I knew that he lived alone, that he was a widower and that, though he had the reputation of having been a ladies' man, he'd had only one wife and mourned her loss greatly. The niece, who let me in and out, was more inclined to chat, but never for more than a sentence or two. It was tacitly understood that her uncle would not approve of our exchanging confidences.

One day Jadlowker announced that he now felt ready to give a recital. From that day on we met more frequently and discussed the suitability of each song for the planned program as we went over it. In putting together his program, Jadlowker always chose the opening and closing songs for each group first; after these were set, he dealt with what came between. There his considerations were contrast and variety of mood, tempo and even key. He often consulted me, but the final choice was truly his.

When the chief selections had been chosen, he said he would sing the entire German group—it was substantial—in Hebrew. "But why?" I asked.

"I want my audience to understand what I am singing," Jadlowker answered, "and I don't like to sing in Hitler's language."

I wanted to say that the language itself was not our enemy, only the man, but I knew that his convictions were strong, that a different opinion from someone so young might be resented and that his point of singing in a language his audience understood was certainly important.

A nonpolitical argument would have been that vocal music should be sung in the language in which it was written. In the United States we generally subscribe to this approach, and there is much to be said in favor of it. After all, vocal music is derived from language, at least rhythmically, and there is more to language than the meaning of the words alone, something one might call national flavor. Of course one can translate "C'est l'extase langoureuse" as "This is languishing ecstasy," but what Englishman or

American would say that? Its flavor is quintessentially French. Or take Heine's "Ich grolle nicht." It means "I hold no grudge" or "I am not angry," but neither quite conveys the sentiment expressed in *Dichterliebe* ("The Poet's Love"). When you consider that the translator of the text also has to match the exact number of syllables, avoid unsingable short vowels—there are many of them in the English language—on high or long notes and cope with a variety of lesser restrictions, it is no wonder that the result often has a meaning quite different from the original. Sometimes the translator even tries to use rhyme. Once, as a Juilliard student sitting at a desk seat at the old Metropolitan Opera in New York, I had a wonderful time comparing the French and English translations of *Götterdämmerung* with each other and with Wagner's German. They were utterly different. Even the title seems absurd in French: *Crépuscule des Dieux;* there is no twilight of the gods on the French scene.

The drawback of a singer's employing the original language is that the audience is so busy reading the translations in the program that they forget to listen to the music. Three thousand people turning a page at the same time make a hideous crackling sound, and it usually happens during a poetic piano postlude, which is particularly resented by accompanists.

Whichever side of this argument you are on, Jadlowker had made his choice. Where no singable translation existed, he commissioned one; there were many poets, young and old, then translating the world's literature into modern Hebrew. Perhaps he also wanted to show his feelings toward his newly adopted country by singing in its language, which had so recently been revived and turned into a modern, spoken tongue.

We needed several additional rehearsals for Jadlowker to learn the Hebrew texts and memorize them. Eventually a date for the concert was set, and it was time for me to buy the first tuxedo of my life, a big moment. I asked my sister to come up from her agricultural school to finger the material—good English worsted—just as you would have your older brother come with you to kick the tires of your first car. When I put that stiff detachable collar on my shirt, it reminded me of the wedding pictures of my parents. I had never thought I would ever be so attired.

The concert was to take place in Haifa, an industrial port city looked down upon by the more cultured Jerusalemites. Later we were to give the same program at the Tel Aviv Museum, in Jerusalem and in some smaller places. At that time Haifa had no concert hall, so the manager who scheduled and arranged our concert had rented a movie house— a huge, ugly place meant to be visited only in the dark. The afternoon of the concert we went to Haifa in a taxi— Palestine was not a large country—and changed into our dress suits backstage. If Jadlowker found the facilities primitive compared with what he had been used to, he never showed it. At eight-thirty sharp, he walked out on the stage, with me a few steps behind.

The name Jadlowker must have meant something to the inhabitants of Haifa, for the house was completely filled. He acknowledged the warm greeting with a slight nod of his head, then turned to me. I played the introduction to the old Italian aria he had chosen to open the program, and he sang it quite *sotto voce.* He needs to warm up a little, I thought. Next came a Handel aria. I played the opening *ritornello* and he did not come in when he should have. I played it again and he came in two bars too soon. Was it possible for a singer of his experience to suffer from stage fright? If so, he overcame it quickly and sang his German group, Schubert, Schumann, Brahms and Mahler, all in Hebrew. When we walked offstage after these for a brief interval, he thanked me for having covered up his mishap in the Handel.

The next piece on the program was Lensky's aria from Tchaikovsky's opera *Eugene Onegin,* a lengthy and beautiful piece of music that encompasses a wide variety of moods and emotions. It was only then that I began to see who Jadlowker had been and who he still was. In front of two thousand pairs of eyes he *became* Lensky, transforming that ugly hall into an elegant European opera house with the sheer magic of his personality. So totally was I under the spell of Jadlowker's dramatic power, conviction and intensity that I quite forgot where I was and what I was supposed to do. I was so overwhelmed, in fact, that I forgot to play at one point and simply stared at him. He turned around to look at me sternly, and I began to play again. This has never happened to me since—not on a stage. When Jadlowker finished the aria there was that moment of absolute silence which shows that an audience has been deeply moved, and then came thunderous applause, shouts of "Bravo!" and relief from the tension in which he had held them for so long.

After the concert everyone present, it seemed to me, wanted to tell Jadlowker how much it had meant to them. They also told him where they had last heard him and what he had sung. Many spoke to him in German, some in Russian and a few in Hebrew. Several people buttonholed me to tell me how lucky I was to be so near greatness at such a tender age. I did not need to be told.

When everyone had left, the manager took us to our hotel, the old Zion Hotel, halfway up Mount Carmel. For some reason a single room had been reserved for us, with two large beds right next to each other. I did not like the idea of sleeping practically in the same bed with the old man, but neither of us was thinking of retiring just then. Jadlowker put on his silk-brocade pajamas—the most elabo-rate ones I had ever seen—and walked up and down the room, just as he had done at all our rehearsals. Much too elated and excited to sleep, he was Kaiser Wilhelm's Lohen-grin again. He spoke of Richard Strauss, Gustav Mahler and even Brahms, for whom he had sung as a youth. He said that Strauss, under whose baton he had sung often, was a thorough, accurate conductor, on whom one could absolutely rely. Perhaps he was a little too matter-of-fact; Jadlowker had seen him play cards during the intermission of a concert, and I gathered from his tone of voice that he did not approve. Mahler, on the other hand, was much more emotional, both in his music-making and in his dealings with people. He was also superstitious and occasionally gave a penny to his singers before a performance for good luck.

I wanted to hear more about Brahms. It seemed quite unreal that I should be in the same room, almost in the same bed, with a man who had sung for Brahms. By now Jadlowker had settled in his bed. "Brahms had a large potbelly," he said, "and he kept his foot on the pedal a lot." I had not played much Brahms, but the thought did occur to me that a protruding belly might account for why the left and right hands in his piano writing often seemed so far apart. The detail about the pedal did not surprise me.

I had never heard Jadlowker speak so much and so freely, and I did not want him to ever stop talking. Through listening to him I felt that somehow I knew these men myself—men who until then had been just names in books and on the title pages of printed music. I also felt that through having made music with Jadlowker, I had entered into a chain of musical continuity, and that if someday I was to tell this to someone else, he or she would also become part of it.

"How did you happen to sing for Brahms?" I asked. "You must have been very young at the time."

"I was indeed," Jadlowker said, "not much older than you are now. And I not only sang *for* him, I sang *with* him. He actually played for me. I was studying voice in Vienna at the time. My teacher was Dr. Gänsbacher—you wouldn't know his name—who was a personal friend of Brahms's, and one day he dropped in when I was in the middle of a voice lesson. Gänsbacher told him he thought I had a future, and Brahms asked to hear me. After the first song—a Brahms song, of course—he sat down at the piano and played the next one himself."

I knew that this was perhaps my only chance to ask Jadlowker anything I wanted to know. I said, "I know Kaiser Wilhelm made you a *Kammersänger"*—a singer of the imperial chamber—"but when did he call you 'my Lohengrin'?"

"He came onstage after a performance at the Berlin Opera House, put his arm around my shoulder and said to the audience, 'This is my Lohengrin.' "

"Was it your favorite part?"

"Wait a moment," Jadlowker said. "There is more to this story. A year or so later the czar of Russia—Riga was part of Imperial Russia then—came to Berlin on a state visit. There was a performance of *Lohengrin* at the opera house and I was asked to visit the two monarchs in their box during intermission. When I entered the box, the kaiser presented me to the czar. 'This is my Lohengrin,' he said. 'He may be your Lohengrin,' the czar replied, 'but he is still my subject.' "

I wished the evening would go on and on, but suddenly Jadlowker was quiet. When I turned toward him I saw in the dim light that he had fallen asleep.

So, eventually, did I.

5. Juilliard and Accompanying

Sᴇʀɢɪᴜs Kᴀɢᴇɴ died in his sleep while in his mid-fifties. He sighed deeply just once, his wife said, and was gone. She tried to revive him, as did the police when they arrived, but with no success. He had left quietly, without a fuss.

Kagen's entire life had been devoted to vocal music: lieder, chansons, songs, cantatas, airs—everything vocal but opera. He had begun his musical career as an accompanist, first in his native Russia, after the revolution in Berlin, then in Paris and eventually in New York. On this gradual westward trek he had worked with many famous singers— Sembrich, Pinza and others—names I knew only from books. When I met him, he no longer traveled but had settled down to teaching at the Juilliard School and at home. He appeared in concerts only when he accompanied his own students, some of them quite well known, whom he had coached and who interpreted the music they sang the way *he* thought it should be performed.

I walked into Sergius Kagen's vocal repertoire class during my second year at Juilliard. I had arrived in New York in August 1947, after a seventeen-day crossing in a freighter.

We had slept in hammocks in large, ill-ventilated holds, and eaten dehydrated eggs for breakfast and dehydrated meat and potatoes at all other meals, with one fresh apple a day —to avoid scurvy, I presume. It was the only shipping available to civilians so soon after the war.

The British had quickly demobilized Palestinians, as we were then called. They knew that Jewish Palestine wanted independence and was willing to fight for it, and now that the war against Germany was over they did not trust us anymore. They were right not to; most of us spent the weeks or months after the end of the war trying to "liberate" arms for the Jewish defense forces, which had no legal ways of acquiring them. As a result, I found myself back in Jerusalem much sooner than anticipated, wearing my demobilization clothes: a dark blue pin-striped suit, a yellow shirt with a white collar, an ugly green necktie and a brown hat with a narrow rim. In this outfit I must have looked absurd getting off the bus in the hot, dry air of Jerusalem, but it felt good to wear civvies again, no matter how outlandish.

The British did not have anything resembling the American G.I. Bill, but they did assist people in completing their studies if they had really interrupted them, and if they had served for more than three years. I was clearly eligible for such assistance and was looking forward to going to the Royal Academy of Music in London, when I discovered that the academy had no vacancies that year. The authorities then gave me a choice of going either to New York or to

Paris. Would I be writing these notes in French if I had made the other choice?

My demobilization suit was not a success in New York, and a distant cousin who had come to meet my ship took me to Macy's the same afternoon and bought me a gabardine suit.

Soon after my arrival in New York I took my entrance examinations at Juilliard. They were extensive: harmony, counterpoint, ear-training, sight-reading, knowledge of musical literature and the ability to identify styles. When I passed these tests, I was promptly allowed to take second-year examinations, then third-year, then finals. I do not know if there is another school that so proudly and arrogantly trusts only its own judgment as Juilliard does, but I was graduated, so to speak, on the day I entered. Years later, when I sat on those juries myself and three faculty members spent half an hour alone with each applicant, I realized that graduates from famous colleges often know very little, and that occasionally the graduates of small, obscure provincial schools could surprise us with their insight and wisdom, as well as their musicality.

For me that day of examinations was exhausting, though of course the results were gratifying. Nevertheless, I still miss the experience so many of my friends talk about, of having gone to college and all that goes with it.

While there were several young composition teachers at Juilliard, I chose to work with an older man, Frederick Jacobi, a teacher of taste and knowledge who realized that

I was quite formed in many ways, but needed advice and help in refining and sharpening certain aspects of my craft.

As a graduate student I also worked with Dr. Robert Tangeman on early music, of which I knew little—as a practicing musician one rarely encountered pre-Bach music in those days—and with Julius Herford, Robert Shaw's mentor, in a course on Bach. Both were excellent teachers, though quite different in approach. With Tangeman the class went over a great many pieces, whereas Herford spent an entire semester on a single Bach cantata, two different, but equally valid approaches.

William Schuman was then president of Juilliard, and under his guidance the school had instituted a new way of teaching musical theory. It was called Literature and Materials of Music, and instead of teaching harmony, counterpoint, orchestration and analysis as separate drills and disciplines totally unrelated to performed music, it attempted to combine these elements into a single system leading to a better understanding of music. Students were made to write, but not exercises; rather, stylistic imitations of compositional techniques: baroque fugal expositions, classical variation and romantic development techniques, polytonal and twelve-tone pieces, for example. Similar methods are now being used in much of the country, but in 1947 the concept was new. I was very excited about it and glad I had chosen Juilliard and not Paris, where, as I discovered during a visit in 1952, I would not have fitted well into Madame Boulanger's circle.

One of Schuman's ways of achieving his goal was to have theory taught only by composers. He believed—and I agree with him—that composers, having gone through the experience themselves, have a different way of explaining to students how a musical composition comes into being than do musicologists, who tend to treat the written page as a document; or than theoreticians, who try to find inner connections, even where none were intended. Since Juilliard is primarily a school for potential performers, the composer's approach to musical analysis is probably the most useful.

Juilliard had also instituted a fellowship program to train graduate students in the new system. I was given one of those fellowships during my second year, and while I was assigned to a composer-teacher as his assistant, I was also expected to observe other teachers, particularly specialists in such fields as vocal or piano repertoire.

On the day I walked into Sergius Kagen's class he was working on the fourth song of *Dichterliebe,* the Schumann song cycle I had often played with Jadlowker. A student was reading the Heine poem:

> *Wenn ich in deine Augen seh',*
> *So schwindet all' mein Leid und Weh;*

after which Kagen corrected his pronunciation. Then another student made a word-by-word translation:

When I into your eyes look,
Then disappears all my grief and woe;

Kagen insisted that his pupils know the meaning of each word. Thus none of the many available translations were of any use to the student, who even had to follow German syntax.

The next four lines of Heine's poem express similar sentiments, but the last two lines take a strange turn:

But when you say: I love you!
Then I must weep bitterly.

A lengthy debate ensued among the students about those lines. Why did he weep when she said, "I love you"? Because it was not true? Because she did not mean it? Because he knew it could not happen? One student even evolved the theory that as long as she was a distant ideal, he could adore her, but the moment she declared her love he lost interest and wept. Kagen listened for a while, then went to the piano and played the passage as Schumann had set it to music. On "I love you" Schumann had composed a suspension resolving into a minor chord, whereas on "I must weep bitterly" he had written an unexpected major cadence.

"No matter how *you* interpret the text," Kagen told the class, "what really matters, the *only* thing that matters, is how *Schumann* interprets it. That and that alone will tell you how to sing the passage." The students and I understood that he had defined an essential point in the interpretation of vocal music.

After class Kagen and I chatted and I told him how Jadlowker had sung a certain passage in *Dichterliebe*. He wanted to hear it, so I went to the piano and played. He did not like Jadlowker's way, said so, and we continued to talk for a long while. Later I was told that he went straight to the dean's office after our session and asked that I become his assistant. I did so, and we became friends.

Kagen knew the vocal repertoire better than anyone else I have met, and made editions of vocal music from Purcell to Debussy—not in order to make money but simply to have them available and to replace incorrect or bad editions. In the world of published music, once a piece is printed, even one by, say, Mozart, it gets reprinted year after year with the same mistakes because no one ever checks it again. Whenever Kagen came across something suspicious in a piece of printed music, something that seemed out of style or too repetitious for its composer, he would return to the manuscript to check. Often he found mistakes, some in well-known, much-performed music, reprinted many times.

Kagen also contributed many new editions of baroque music, where the original had only the vocal line and a figured bass and some ambitious editor had devised fussy,

overly ornate right-hand accompaniments that infuriated
Kagen. If the faulty edition was the only one available, there
was really nothing for him to do but bring out his own,
marked by simplicity and fidelity to the spirit of the original.

Sergius Kagen lived in one of those old buildings on
West End Avenue that are soundproof not by design but
because of the solidity of the building materials used. Many
musicians live in this area, performers who in spite of their
fame or income would never be tolerated in one of those
modern high-rise buildings where details of your neighbor's
sex life and bathroom habits are clearly audible, and where
a piano or strong voice would be heard through six stories.
The old buildings, Kagen explained, had a foot of air space
between the ceiling of one apartment and the floor of the
one above it. I never checked on this, but it was certainly
quiet in his apartment and one could play the piano at all
hours without disturbing anyone.

We spent many evenings together, looking at music,
playing it or simply talking. Kagen pointed out to me how
Purcell, whose vocal music I had not known before, sets
such words as *woe* or *joy,* not through tone-painting in the
accompaniment but in the voice alone, through expressive
melisma or coloratura. We agreed that words and music
seem to go perfectly together in Schubert; that Schumann
sometimes continued his melodies in the piano when he ran
out of text; that Brahms occasionally imposed his strong

melodies on the text even when they went against the natural accents of language; and that Hugo Wolf, on the other hand, always shaped his vocal line to fit the declamation of the text. Kagen also introduced me to the songs of Fauré, and we compared settings by him and by Debussy of the same poems. Of living composers he admired Samuel Barber and Benjamin Britten, who, like Purcell, followed the natural inflections of the English language. I began to understand how language influences and shapes music, and that if there are national characteristics in music, they derive from language. Kagen also pointed out that nations with strong folk music, such as Spain and Ireland, have produced few art songs.

We also talked about the art of accompanying and eventually took a few pianists into the vocal repertoire class, where they learned to sight-read because of the sheer quantity of music they had to play every week. In a separate class I taught them to transpose, to "realize" figured bass—that is, to translate numbers into chords on a keyboard—and thus play a baroque *continuo* part, to play from a full orchestral score and to acquire other allied skills.

The life of the accompanist is a strange one. He spends as much time on the stage as the artist whom he accompanies, he wears the same outlandish nineteenth-century costume, but at the party after the concert someone will come up to him and say: "You played beautifully. By the way, what is your name?" Yet for many years I supplemented my income by accompanying. When you are young and in need of money, you have to accompany all kinds of people. I once toured with a baritone who abstained from sex the night before a concert because he thought it debilitating. But after his performance he had to have a woman, and he went to great lengths to prearrange this—not always easy while on tour. I also remember a mezzo-soprano who expected services beyond music from her accompanist. She was so well known for this that hotel reservations were always made for only one room with a large bed. When I, faithful to my young wife, asked for a room of my own, I was frowned upon and not reengaged.

I had entered this field first by becoming the second accompanist at the Jerusalem radio station. The first accompanist had the right to make up the schedule, so if a violinist was to play a Beethoven sonata, he took him; if a folksinger came with his own "material," I got him. These folksingers often brought little scraps of paper with a melody barely scratched on them, and I was expected to make up an accompaniment in the mood and style of the song. The rehearsal would be just before the broadcast, and sometimes the singer would get nervous and, just as the On the Air sign went on, would whisper in my ear, "I don't think I can reach that high note today. Please play the whole song a step lower." One had little choice but to smile and do it. Even good singers don't always rehearse all their encores, and sometimes, when the concert went particularly well, I was handed a song I'd never seen, right on stage, as the fifth encore. These songs were often showy numbers and therefore difficult to play, but no one in the audience was supposed to know that I was sight-reading.

I did not play only for singers. With violinists and cellists one can play longer, more sustained pieces—sonatas and concerti—but instrumentalists are no less idiosyncratic than singers. For a while I toured the American South with a European violinist who believed that outside of New York all food was inedible and probably dangerous. Wherever we went, he locked himself in his hotel room and ordered boiled eggs and toast from room service, the only items he considered safe. He drove a large Cadillac he was very fond of, and when interviewing me, he showed more interest in my ability to drive than to play the piano.

Another violinist I traveled with was afraid of overtiring himself and had his accompanist play a solo of about fifteen minutes just after intermission. When I asked whether I could play my own music, he said I could play whatever I wanted, as long as it did not last more than fifteen minutes. One evening, in a small town in Western Canada, I'd had too many drinks with my dinner, and while I could get through his part of the program with crossed hands—we had performed the same program many times together—I was in the mood to improvise when it came to my solo. Why not? The program simply listed my music and no one knew it. I must have become quite excited that night, because when I came offstage the worried violinist asked, "Are you sick? What on earth is the matter with you?" After convincing him that I was well by playing the rest of the program without faltering, I fell into bed in my hotel. The next morning in the local paper I read one of the finest reviews I've ever had: "The pianist produced sounds which this reviewer did not know existed." I wish I knew what I played that night.

Kagen and I agreed that one of the worst aspects of the life of an accompanist is the constant travel. Not only the time spent in public transportation but also that spent in hotel rooms in strange towns is time wasted. Hindemith prided himself on being able to compose anywhere and at any time, whether on trains or in hotels. I cannot do this; I need some continuity of thought, so a day off in some strange town could not be used positively. After a while all strange towns began to look alike: Woolworth's to the left, Rexall's to the right, and a large Sears sign opposite. Once I remember buying a local newspaper just to find out where I was.

Kagen, who was more devoted to vocal music than I and later gave voice lessons himself, often spoke about the strange goings-on in the studios of voice teachers. Some famous singers begin to teach when they reach a certain age, but often they are what is called "natural" talents and so cannot explain or analyze what they do so well. When a student has a problem, such singers simply sing the passage for the student and then say, "That's how you do it." At least this does no harm, even if it does not teach the student anything.

Among singing teachers there are at least as many different approaches and systems as among teachers of piano. Each believes only in his own system, and for a student to switch teachers often means starting anew. Yet sometimes they have to do it, when serious vocal problems prevent progress or, in extreme cases, when they lose their voice altogether. Even professional singers remain under the supervision of a teacher well into their careers, so a strong dependence evolves, stronger than in any other field of music.

Not all that goes on in voice studios is well-intentioned or competent. I knew one voice teacher who hit his students' Adam's apple when he disliked their sound. One of Kagen's favorite stories about charlatans among singing teachers concerned a man who put his students flat on their back, straddled them and then bounced up and down, purportedly to improve the functioning of their diaphragm. One of his students was a nun, and when he tried the maneuver on her, she reported him to the head of that school and he was fired.

Besides his books on vocal music, Sergius Kagen wrote songs himself, tasteful settings of carefully chosen poetry in impeccable taste and prosody. He did not approve of the unusual demands that were beginning to be made by some

composers, and did not permit his students to sing compositions that went far above or below the natural range of their
voices, or that made them howl, growl, squeak, grunt or
wheeze in those distortions then becoming fashionable with
the avant-garde.

Kagen disliked the term "avant-garde" in reference to the
arts. "Avant-garde is a military term," he would say. "It
refers to the advance guard, which is sent into enemy territory to scout it in secret. If they find the situation suitable,
the whole army follows; if not, they withdraw. In our day
and age," he would continue sternly, "the advance guard has
gone into enemy territory and simply remained there, although no one has followed them except for the press,
which needs new material constantly, and some misguided
foundations afraid to miss a potentially significant advance
in musical culture."

In Kagen's day the avant-garde was mostly studious,
joyless and intentionally incomprehensible. He died before
later avant-garde trends made musicians wear masks, walk
about the stage, speak and count in languages they did not
know and belabor the piano with feathers inside and ham-
mers from below. I wonder what he would have made of
it all. He died also before interest in vocal music, other than
nineteenth-century opera sung by superstars, diminished; in
his time there were several vocal recitals each week in New
York.

These days, when I walk near Lincoln Center, and a music student carrying a volume of Purcell or Debussy songs with Sergius Kagen's name on the cover passes me, I see only Kagen's name. The student probably does not know it is there.

6. William Steinberg

William Steinberg was a musician's musician: solely devoted to music and neither showy nor self-centered. Musicians who played under him—or rather, with him—in Pittsburgh and Boston, where I had occasion to meet them, knew that they were not being used simply to further his glory. He never made impossible demands and never ridiculed them in front of their colleagues; when they had difficulties, he helped them. Even today, playing in an orchestra often means being exposed to the whims of a tyrant, and in some orchestras unpleasant tensions reign, to the extent that members of such orchestras consider music-making a duty, even a chore. With Steinberg one always had the feeling that the goal was a blending of many individual talents into a musical whole.

Steinberg, who came from the Central European tradition, always included something recent in his programs and was loyal to composers he believed in. He played Schönberg and Mahler regularly long before these two—in particular Mahler—became staples of the repertoire.

Conductors who are music directors make up the programs. Guest conductors submit theirs but are on occasion told to play something else, for when a music director is pressured into performing a certain composition, he may turn it over to one of his guest conductors. Orchestra musicians know instinctively whether a piece they are rehearsing has behind it the love and conviction of the maestro or whether he is conducting it as an obligation.

A composer depends totally upon the performer in order to be heard at all and to have his ideas and intentions realized (unless he composes directly on recording tape or into a computer). If he wants to reach the audience that goes to symphony concerts, only conductors can help him achieve this.

Some composers, especially those who studied for many years at a university and then went directly into teaching without ever having experienced "real" life, ignore the orchestral world altogether—perhaps they find it impossible to reach it—and are content to write for the "contemporary ensemble" that almost every university now has. If their own school has such an ensemble, they are in a position to invite similarly situated composers to present *their* works, which in turn leads to invitations for them; thus, they travel and lead fairly contented lives within this limited sphere of activity. University poets seem to have similar reciprocal arrangements and spend much time traveling and reading their poems. The introductions some of these poets give are often longer and more entertaining than the poems they eventually read; the university composers' program notes are also long, but rarely more entertaining than the compositions they accompany.

I have never been drawn to this world and have no regrets, although I know that the people who run it are members of all the influential committees, the ones that distribute money in the form of prizes, awards and grants. I have always preferred performers who wanted to play my music solely because they liked it, not because I could return a favor—or, for that matter, because I am Viennese, contemporary, American, not a woman, Jewish, or for any other extraneous, nonmusical reason.

The personal relationship between composer and performer can be intimate, friendly, casual or nonexistent. Once a piece of music is published, anyone can buy it and do whatever he likes with it: play it too slow, too fast, too loud, too soft, straightforwardly or erratically. Writers sometimes ask whether a composer's relationship to his listener is comparable to theirs with an unknown reader. What the two have in common is that each must be based on sympathy and understanding; beyond that they are different in essence. An author speaks to his reader directly, without any intermediary. The reader, one supposes, compares people and situations described in the book with similar experiences in his own life, and if the book tells him something new or deep, he is enriched. Of course no two readers get the same meaning from a book, even though words are much more precise in conveying information than musical sounds are. No two people ever hear the same thing in a piece of music either, but the composer cannot speak to his listener directly; he must have an intermediary, a performer. Further, the listener, especially when exposed to a new piece, must take that particular performer's interpretation as the true one, since he has nothing with which to compare it.

Writers almost never see their readers actually reading their books, and painters meet their audiences only at openings and shows. Only the composer can sit among several hundred people and observe them responding to his sounds at the very moment they are hearing them.

Analogies are constantly drawn between the arts, though their differences are actually greater than their similarities. In recent times, for instance, the avant-garde has been singularly successful in the world of painting, so much so that many painters have become enormously rich. There truly *is* a market for new paintings. In writing, on the other hand, there never has been much of an avant-garde movement; words are too universally necessary to lend themselves to much experimentation. In serious music, where there is little money to be made, the avant-garde was at first so mathematical that it held interest only for other practitioners; then it went to the other extreme, in aleatory music, which almost abandoned the function of the composer by leaving everything to chance. The wider public became alienated and is now suspicious of everything new.

The only other art in which there is an interpreter between the creator and the audience is the theater, and there the leeway given to actor and director is even greater than in music. Imprecise though it is, music notation does tell the performer the exact rhythmic sequence and precise pitches he is to produce, whereas the actor, guided by his director, can speak lines at his own speed, raise or lower his voice at will and take whatever time he wants to get from one spot on stage to another. There is no way that the written word, called "precise" only a few paragraphs ago, can convey the playwright's wishes to the actor exactly in every detail.

To return to music: the composer rarely can choose his performer, and it is the performer who decides what to play. There are a number of reasons for an instrumentalist to play a new work. Young players often try to put a premiere on their programs because they know it will attract the press. Established artists consider it to their advantage to occasionally give their public something unusual; it makes them seem adventuresome and enterprising. Some performers have a favorite living composer and play his new works, as he writes them, over the years. Such a relationship is most satisfying to the composer; I was lucky to have had it with William Steinberg, David Bar-Illan and others.

There are also performers who specialize in presenting a certain type of new music. They are extraordinarily capable in technical aspects, though often lacking in expressiveness. Difficulty per se attracts them—music itself really bores them—and they are happiest when they can play eleven notes in the left hand against thirteen in the right with absolute rhythmic accuracy. Our century has produced a number of composers who provide these musicians with material whose chief attraction is its difficulty. ("There are only two other groups in the whole world who can play this piece" is what such players often tell you.) Having mastered one piece of almost insurmountable difficulty, they move on to the next. The deepening of understanding that comes from long acquaintance with the expressive content of a piece holds no interest for them—if only because the music they play usually does not contain that element; the longer one knows it, the less interesting it becomes.

Equally deplorable are performers who won't play anything later than Brahms, Debussy or wherever they draw their line, for their attitude will kill the very thing they aim to preserve. Any art that is not permitted to grow, even by trial and error, is doomed to wither eventually.

To me the ideal performer is the one who presents the new along with the tried and proven. Thus he exposes new music to the large audience that eventually matters, rather than to the small coterie that attends festivals of novelties. I have always preferred to have my music presented in this way and have deliberately shunned the other.

The ideal performer not only plays one's music as was

intended, but adds a quality that enhances it. When I sat recently in Boston's Symphony Hall and listened to Itzhak Perlman play my violin concerto, which was written for him, I was overwhelmed by the nuances his interpretation added. I tried to define what made his performance so extraordinary. His technical prowess is known, as is the beauty of his sound (it "emanates directly from his soul," I wrote in the program notes); his well-known physical handicap must also have given him inner strength. In the end I decided that his secret was that he had retained the quality and the purity of the child in him. Just a few days earlier, at a dinner in the house of the composer Earl Kim, Itzhak had entertained their child by making sounds with his fist on the back of his head, varying the pitch by opening or closing his mouth. Suddenly he turned toward me, smiled and "played" one of the themes of my concerto that way.

The first performer ever to play my music in public was Zvi Zeitlin, also a violinist. I met him through Hermann Jadlowker, who one year chose to do a Mozart aria that called for a violin obbligato. Later I met Zvi again when we were both in British uniform during World War II and were delegated, after some months of routine military service in North Africa, to play serious music for British and Allied troops. We were sent to such unlikely places as oil fields in Iraq and Iran, little islands on the Persian Gulf and off the coast of Saudi Arabia—wherever there were airfields or garrisons with men dying of boredom. For two weeks we even entertained Soviet troops, in return for a concert visit by a Russian violin-piano team. Our audiences were often small—there was no pretense that we would offer pop entertainment—but always grateful. Zvi knew that I was composing in secret and urged me to write a sonata for violin and piano. When I did, we played it at the American University in Cairo, and the next morning I found myself taken seriously by the English and French papers, which were read by the large European population of Cairo. Later that year we played the sonata in many more places. At the time I was only nineteen years old, and this gave me much encouragement and impetus to continue.

I was almost thirty when my music was first played by a major orchestra. I was living in New York, touring as an accompanist and teaching some classes at Juilliard. I had not joined the modern-music establishment—I still have not—and felt lonely and miserable. One evening I wrote a letter to Dimitri Mitropoulos, music director of the New York Philharmonic. To my surprise my phone rang two days later and a deep voice said, "This is Mitropoulos." At first I thought one of my friends was playing a practical joke on me. He asked me to come see him at the Great Northern Hotel the following evening; he lived in a modest apartment on its top floor, practically next door to Carnegie Hall. He asked me to play my score for him and when I

Practicing my first publicly performed composition with the violinist Zvi Zeitlin

finished—the piece was called Prelude and Rondo Giocoso —he took out his calendar and said, "I will play this on October fifteenth." Very few conductors will commit themselves so quickly. He said nice things to me after the concert, but what was more important, when David Bar-Illan proposed my second piano concerto to him the following year, he accepted it without even seeing the score. There is no higher sign of confidence a conductor can give a composer.

Conversely, the highest sign of confidence a composer can give a conductor is to trust him to rehearse a new piece on his own. When Gerard Schwarz premiered a work of mine in Los Angeles in October 1983 and I had another premiere elsewhere the night before, I could not attend any of his rehearsals. Yet the performance was perfect; all the tempi, phrasings and dynamics were right, as I knew they would be.

Between my encounters with Mitropoulos and Schwarz, I had others with a number of conductors, including Bernstein, Leinsdorf and Comissiona, but none evolved into the lasting musical relationship I shared with William Steinberg. I call it a musical relationship because it was never intimate, or even what might be termed one of friendship. Steinberg was a reserved man. He ate dinner only once in my house, and when I saw him in Pittsburgh or Boston we spoke only about music. I knew he loved his wife and suffered greatly when she died, but he rarely spoke of her.

We never even called each other by our first names, but this may have been European reticence; in fact, I knew no one who called him Bill or even William.

I spent the winter of 1964–65 in Rome, and during that year Steinberg performed my *Concerto a Tre* in Pittsburgh. It is a work for solo clarinet, trumpet and trombone that I had written ten years earlier for Thomas Scherman and the now defunct Little Orchestra Society. Generally it is played whenever a conductor chooses to feature his first clarinet, trumpet and trombone players as soloists. My publishers got a positive report from Pittsburgh and suggested that I offer Steinberg the premiere of a new orchestral piece on which I was working. He responded favorably, and the following year I traveled to Pittsburgh to attend the rehearsals and premiere of my *Mutabili: Variants for Orchestra,* later recorded by the Louisville Orchestra.

It was then that I met Steinberg personally, and I knew, as rehearsals began, that he would perform my music with the same devotion, attention to detail and positive attitude that he gave classical masters. I also felt that he genuinely liked my music, and although no oral or written agreement was ever made, thereafter I traveled to Pittsburgh almost every year—certainly every other year—for a premiere. At that time the Pittsburgh Orchestra played in the Syria Mosque—this was before Heinz Hall had been refurbished—and I stayed at an old-fashioned hotel almost next door and made friends with Frederick Dorian, author and

With William Steinberg after a concert at Carnegie Hall
WHITESTONE PHOTO

musicologist, who wrote excellent program notes for the orchestra. Over the years Steinberg premiered my Third Symphony, my Concerto for Violin, Cello and Orchestra and the symphonic version of *Samson Agonistes,* which he also conducted with the New York Philharmonic, the Chicago Symphony and other orchestras.

Whenever I arrived in Pittsburgh I would call Steinberg to say hello and find out the rehearsal schedule. Once when he answered the phone he said brusquely, "Do you know what I am doing? I am studying your *wrong* metronome indications." I'd had trouble in this area before. "Please ignore them," I answered, "and trust your musical judgment." Metronome markings are the only precise way to indicate the tempo at which a piece of music is to be performed. The metronome was invented in Beethoven's time—earlier periods were satisfied with such indications as *tempo giusto* (the right tempo)—and he must have had a hard time with it. Even today arguments rage over whether his metronome did not work properly or whether he really meant some of his improbable indications.

I too have always had a difficult time with the metronome. On days when I feel sprightly and full of energy, I tend to mark faster tempi than at times when a haze hangs over the atmosphere or my soul. I also know that a tempo that is right for a man alone in a small room may be quite wrong for an orchestra in a hall seating three thousand people. Yet performers and publishers like to see metronome indications. These days I will put down an indication like "quarter note equals 66–72," thus allowing leeway for temperamental decisions and moods of the moment.

Altogether the question of how detailed the markings should be that a composer inserts in his music is a puzzling one. Music students love the story of Robert Schumann putting *presto possibile* (as fast as possible)—only to mark later *più presto* (faster). Apparently extreme precision in markings began with Debussy. Certainly Bartók was serious about it when he put a precise timing at the end of each section of a piece. I have found that when I put *poco ritardando* and *poco accelerando* signs in my music, performers tend to overlook the word *poco* (a little), and slow down or speed up enormously. Such indications were meant only to delineate musical phrasing. If, on the other hand, I mark minimally, pedantic, letter-perfect performers will play everything at the same tempo, absolutely straight and say self-righteously, "I always respect the composer's wishes." Is there an answer to this? Not really. Good musicians will know what to do; they always find the "right" tempo. Others will not, no matter how many markings there are in the score.

Some people speak of a "definitive performance," but there really is no such thing. Two quite different performances of the same work can be equally valid. The joy of musical life is that no two performances are *ever* exactly alike. The notion of the definitive performance has been encouraged by the makers and sellers of phonograph records. Once a performance is recorded, it is immutably frozen forever. Artists such as Schnabel and Kreisler treated a recording simply as a record—no pun intended—of a single performance. They did not even mind releasing recordings with mistakes on them, as long as they had the flow and continuity of a real performance. Nowadays recordings consist of so many splicings that perfection is seemingly attained, but it is really the skill of the recording engineer rather than of the artist that makes this perfection possible. During the years I taught at Juilliard I often encountered students who had come to New York from far away and who heard for the first time in live concert an artist they had admired on recordings. "He hit a wrong note," they would say, quite shocked. Yes, they all hit wrong notes sometimes, thank God; only recordings are perfect.

Only once did William Steinberg telephone me. It was so unusual that I waited patiently to hear the reason. It came out slowly, delicately and indirectly: he thought there was something wrong with the ending of my Third Symphony, a score I had sent him recently. I got out the music, turned to the last pages and listened carefully to what he had to say. Near the end of the piece I had speeded up the tempo until there was only one beat per measure and then had ended on what would be perceived as an inconclusive upbeat. Steinberg was right. As he pointed out, Beethoven was fond of fast tempi, with only one beat per measure, but his markings *a tre battute* or *a quattro battute* showed that he knew their groupings must still be counted. I changed the ending to have the last measure on a downbeat, and when I heard the piece was glad I had done so.

In 1969, when Steinberg conducted my Concerto for Violin, Cello and Orchestra with the Boston Symphony, I arrived the evening before the first rehearsal. Steinberg took me to dinner and announced, "You are going to get a bad review tomorrow."

I have had my share of bad reviews, but never had I been told in advance that I would receive one. "How do you know?" I asked.

"The local critic has attacked me for not playing enough local composers," he answered. "It is logical for him to prove tomorrow that you are unworthy."

He was right; the local man outdid himself in vituperation. (It was in this same double concerto, incidentally, that Michael Tilson Thomas, then assistant conductor to Steinberg, made his conducting debut at Avery Fisher Hall, when Steinberg was suddenly taken ill in the middle of a concert.)

When a work involved soloists, as did the double concerto, Steinberg liked me to play a piano rehearsal with the soloists, usually the day before the first orchestra rehearsal. The purpose was for the soloists to get acquainted with each other as well as with the music, and perhaps for Steinberg to hear my own tempi. Seiji Ozawa also asked me to play a piano rehearsal with Itzhak Perlman when he performed my violin concerto with the Boston Symphony. Ozawa was kind enough to compliment me on my piano playing, even though he caught me playing a phrase differently from the way I had written it. "Shall we play what you are playing, or what you have written?" he asked tactfully. I realized instantly that I had made a mistake in notating that phrase.

Even such a natural act as playing in one's own piano rehearsal can lead to trouble. When I arrived at the piano rehearsal for *Journals of a Songmaker,* which called for a soprano and a baritone, I noticed a young woman in the hall. The moment I stepped to the piano, she got up and left angrily. I did not pay much attention, since I was intent on working with the singers, but later that evening I had a phone call from her, and she was angry. "I am the staff pianist of the Pittsburgh Symphony," she said. "I have practiced your piece for weeks, and you know it isn't easy. Then you just come in and play it yourself." I could do nothing but apologize.

Many people believe that composers are the best interpreters of their own music. I don't believe this is necessarily so—and certainly not in my case. I do play the piano in public, mostly chamber music and accompaniments, but my efforts in conducting have not been successful. Some years ago I was asked to conduct a chorus in a work of mine. Someone else had prepared the singers, and they knew the music; all I had to do was start them and keep

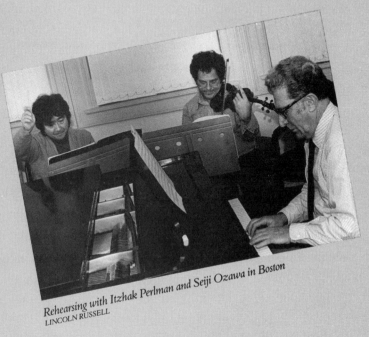

Rehearsing with Itzhak Perlman and Seiji Ozawa in Boston
LINCOLN RUSSELL

them together. I climbed up on the podium, raised my hands, then lowered them, but nobody sang. I tried it again, and this time a few of them came in but by no means all. On another occasion I conducted an orchestra, and the music became slower and slower no matter what I did. Finally I stopped and asked the players why they were playing at that tempo. "We're just following your beat," they answered. Since then I have left conducting to those who know how to do it.

William Steinberg's last concert as music director of the Pittsburgh Symphony took place in the newly renovated Heinz Hall, a tasteful blend of the old and the new, with excellent acoustics, which was splendidly festive for the occasion. I had been asked to write a piece for the event and had offered *Journals of a Songmaker*. Even for his last concert Steinberg wanted a *new* work, a significant gesture. I had told Gail Godwin, who had written the text of *Journals of a Songmaker*, several details of my musical relationship with Steinberg, and she had inserted some oblique references to them in the text—that is, they were oblique in the sense that they would have no double meaning for the audience, which was handed the customary printed libretto, but would perhaps be meaningful to Steinberg. I was hoping to hear his reaction to such lines as "You were never good at endings," and he, perceptive man that he was, would surely have made some joking reference to them at the planned after-concert reception.

But Steinberg never came to the reception. He gave an impassioned performance of Beethoven's Ninth Symphony, and the ovation at the end was highly emotional. The orchestra stood up and the standing audience clapped rhythmically. It was an ovation that could have gone on for a long time. I was backstage, quite moved, aware that this was the end of an era of joyous music-making, when I noticed that Steinberg had left the hall and had stepped into the dark side street by the stage door. I wanted to follow him, but when I saw the expression on his face—not sadness, but rather rage, rage that it all was now over—I did not. I should have followed him into that dark alley and dropped all my reticence to tell him that I too did not want it to end, but his expression frightened me. I returned to the hall; he did not.

Some years later I saw that expression again, on the face of a terminally ill woman whose body had become frail but whose spirit was in a rage against her fate.

7. Martha Graham

THE first score I wrote for Martha Graham was eventually called *Samson Agonistes*. At the opening, in April 1961, she had named it "Visionary Recital," but after reworking it extensively before the second season (without any changes in the music) she gave it the other title, and *Samson Agonistes* it has remained. It also became the title of my symphonic version of the same music, which the New York Philharmonic, the Chicago Symphony and others later played.

My first meeting with Martha Graham was a formal occasion at her school. Leroy Leatherman, her manager at the time, told me the size of the orchestra I was to write for and other technical details, then introduced me to her and left us alone. Martha handed me a script, which she asked me not to show to anyone, and waited while I glanced at it. It was not a detailed description of dance sequences but rather her thoughts about the significance and meaning of Samson's story, about strength and weakness, honesty and deceit.

When I looked up from the script, Martha began to speak slowly. She told me that this was to be her first work with a male as the central character and that, though there might be a small part in it for herself, choreographing for a male principal was a new situation for her. I knew that Martha Graham never told a story realistically in movement, but instead dealt with it symbolically or philosophically; however, she did reveal that there would be a scene in which Samson is being taunted or tortured, and that there would be a scene in which he was blinded. As she spoke I began to hear music, and I decided to accompany the taunting-torturing scene with cool, unemotional, slightly jazzy music. I also knew that I would have the blinding, which turned out to be extraordinarily effective theatrically, done in silence. I also spoke to Martha about "ceremonial drumming," a Near Eastern, repetitiously bland kind of drumming with which I was enamored at the time; she liked this idea and thought it would fit.

I knew the work was to be about half an hour long, and before leaving I asked when it should be ready. The question brought the first full smile I had seen on her expressive face. She told me that Paul Hindemith had been commissioned to write a score for her in the 1940s and, when told that she needed it in late spring, had pulled his diary out of his pocket, studied it for a moment and then said, "Madam, you shall have it on May eighteenth." And precisely on May 18 he had knocked at the door of her school, the complete score under his arm. This seemed overly precise to me, as it must have to her to elicit such a smile, but I

decided right then that I would try never to miss the deadline of a commission, particularly if a theater had been
rented and an orchestra hired.

After this I did not see Martha again until I went to play
the completed score of *Samson* for her. It was a tense
moment. As I played I saw in her face that she must be
seeing gestures and movements, just as I had heard sounds
when she spoke. Whenever there was an extended solo she
asked which instrument was to play it, and I began to realize
that her musicality, extraordinary though it is, has nothing
to do with study or with reading music. It really amounts
to an innate understanding of the inner gestures of music.

Our session went well, and the next time I heard my
music was in the theater, with Robert Irving conducting in
the pit and Paul Taylor taunting Bertram Ross to my
sounds in front of Rouben Ter-Arutunian's brilliant set.
The only faux pas I committed on opening night was to go
to the reception, held at Bethsabe de Rothschild's house,
immediately after the last curtain call. I sat in that elegant
house alone, stared at by the servants, until the first guests
and dancers arrived a full hour later.

A few months after the premiere of *Samson* my phone
rang. It was Martha. She had liked the music for *Samson*,
she said; was I free to do another score? Indeed I was. This
time it would be a true collaboration, step by step. Could
I come to Shelter Island for a weekend to talk about the new
work? Indeed I could. There would be the beach, a large

dog and two dancers to entertain my wife and young son, Dan, if they cared to come along. They did.

Shelter Island is near the tip of New York's Long Island. After suburbia there is a pleasant drive through farm country, with a ferry to the island at the end. Martha had rented a house on a large plot, surrounded by tall shade trees. The beach was nearby, and there was indeed a fierce-looking gentle dog and two dancers ready to keep Johanna and Dan entertained.

I saw little of them for the next two days as I sat with Martha in her study and listened to her talk about the new work. It was to be about the lust an older woman feels for a younger man, her husband's son from another marriage. When he rejects her, she betrays him to her husband with a lie by saying that he assaulted her. There is a similar plot in the Bible, the story of the young Joseph and Potiphar's wife, but Martha's work was to be *Phaedra,* a far more tragic story. The work would open with Phaedra—Martha, of course—alone onstage on a bedlike structure that Isamu Noguchi would devise, racked by her lust for Hippolytus, son of Theseus, who would slowly be revealed behind another of Noguchi's structures. Aphrodite would be there too, encouraging Phaedra, and chaste Diana would protect young Hippolytus. The story would be shown twice, both as the lie Phaedra tells Theseus, and as it really happened. From these and other diverse scenes the focus would return to Phaedra alone in that bed with her terrible, unquenchable lust. At this moment I heard a rich orchestral sound with an excited running motif for the trumpet. Later, when I wrote the score, I returned to this motif whenever Phaedra was alone on her bed, thus giving the music a form similar to the dance.

As Martha spoke of lust, the room seemed to be permeated with that emotion. When she spoke of Aphrodite, Artemis and Pasiphaë, the one who loved the bull, she became each of them in turn before my eyes. I also saw that lust was not love in the romantic sense, and certainly not mere sex, which by comparison was merely a physical exercise between consenting partners. Phaedra's lust as described that weekend by Martha was a fever, an illness for which there was only one cure, and when that cure was unattainable, the result could only be death. What powerful women Greek antiquity had! Martha had done her Medea and her Clytemnestra before I knew her, and I was glad that Phaedra was to be mine. She seemed the most human of them all, the most understandable and the most pitiful.

As I listened to Martha, I had a small insight into the depth of her knowledge, experience and wisdom. I also had a sense of artistic union, a feeling one does not often have in collaborations with others and which I have rarely experienced so intensely as on that weekend on Shelter Island.

We must have eaten and drunk, but I have no memory of that. I do remember—who could forget?—that when it was time to leave, little Dan went over to Martha and while

Martha Graham as Phaedra and Paul Taylor as Hippolytus
MARTHA SWOPE

we all thought he was going to hug her, he bit her right in the stomach, the height he could then reach. He must have been furious with the woman who had taken his father away from him so completely on the weekend. Martha laughed—I don't think Dan hurt her—but many years later, when I took him backstage after an evening of the Graham Company, she looked long and hard at him and then asked, "Are you the young man who once bit me in the stomach?"

Everyone present heard it and Dan was mortified. I felt sympathetic, for when I was a boy I had evidently once punched Alfred Adler, with whom my mother was studying psychoanalysis in Vienna, in the stomach in a similar rage.

After the weekend on Shelter Island I began to write *Phaedra* immediately. The moment of lust, as brought to life so vividly by Martha, stayed with me intensely for a long while. Whenever I finished a section I would go see Martha at her New York apartment to play it for her, and then we would talk about the next section. It was a much closer collaboration than sitting alone in one's studio with a script for several months, not knowing whether the result would be suitable until the score was completed. Yet, paradoxically, whereas *Samson* never required a change, *Phaedra* needed some. How delicately Martha went about telling me. The company loved the music, she said; could I come watch a rehearsal? This was unusual; I knew that she never had a composer present when she created a dance work. (The word "choreography," like "orchestration," is used so much as metaphor these days that one hesitates to use it in its original sense.) After delivering the first section of *Phaedra*, I had asked to see a rehearsal. "Would you like me to be present in your room while you compose?" Martha asked. I realized that she must have some special reason for asking me to a rehearsal now. She did. One section of the music was too long for what she had choreographed; another was too short for the dramatic effect she wanted. She wanted me to see this for myself. The cut was easy; the additional music was not. I was deep into another work by then and had difficulty writing the extra interlude. Whenever I see *Phaedra* today, even the recent revival on television, those extra minutes make me wince.

Considerable time elapses between the writing of a piece of music and hearing it performed. Instrumental parts have to be copied, proofread, corrected and photocopied. This gap is a problem for the composer, since by the time rehearsals begin his mind is already involved in writing something else, and the piece being rehearsed belongs to the past. Of course one can get back into the previous mood, but ideally one would like to hear a piece the moment it is finished. In the world of dance this is almost so. Everything is done on a tight schedule. The composer supplies the company with a piano score so that the dancers can begin to work while he does the orchestration. The dancers do not hear the

orchestral version until a day or two before the opening—
which, in turn, can cause them problems. From their rehearsals they are used to the precise attack of the piano, and
when the same music suddenly comes from, say, a muted
violin section, it sounds very different. Still, they adjust
quickly; they have to, since everything happens in a relatively short span of time.

The day before opening night Martha had not yet decided
how Phaedra was to die. The music was not affected, so I
sat in the empty theater and watched her try many different
ways, accompanied only by the rehearsal pianist. Only the
last thirty seconds or so were involved, but they were
crucial. Perhaps I am committing an indiscretion by reveal-
ing that she changed her choreography after opening night.
The timing of so significant a scene cannot really be determined until it has been tried out in front of a full house;
one cannot tell whether it "works," as theater people say,
until it has been exposed to the reaction of a live audience.

In the years since, I have seen a number of dancers in the
part of Phaedra—all strong, powerful dancers—but to me
none has had the conviction or subtlety that Martha dis-
played, particularly in those last thirty seconds when she
kills herself.

Phaedra was first presented in late spring. For the summer
of the same year Martha was committed to creating a new
work for the New London, Connecticut, Festival. There

was no time to write a new score, so she asked me whether I had anything lighthearted to suit a company work without "stars." I proposed my *Concerto a Tre,* the same work that had won me William Steinberg's friendship, and Martha choreographed *Secular Games,* one of her most delightful pieces, to it. Few people know what a delicate sense of humor she has, since she has done so few works that have allowed it to shine. *Secular Games* required many dancers, and since the present Graham company is small, it stayed in the repertory for only a few seasons.

The success or failure of a dance piece rarely depends upon the music. *Samson Agonistes* ceased to exist because that elaborately beautiful set, with its series of vertical poles that suggested purdah, was used, as Graham sets often were, for many different purposes. While the company was on tour abroad, it was discovered that it took the stagehands longer than the usual intermission time to dismantle all those vertical poles, so the piece left the company's repertory, never to return.

During that same tour *Phaedra* became a real *succès de scandale* for the wrong reasons. An American congressman saw it in Frankfurt and stated, in a widely quoted interview, that it was obscene. He probably did not know the difference between the portrayal of lust and pornography, but such are the ways of our world that his pronouncement made *Phaedra* a huge success and every performance in New York was sold out. In fact, I had to stand in the back of the theater to see it that season. All my friends teased me that I had become a composer of obscene music.

The opening-night party for *Phaedra* took place at the Dakota, that marvelously ornate old apartment house on Central Park West. By then I knew that it takes dancers at least an hour to get ready to meet their public, so I wandered about the streets of New York until the proper time. Many playwrights, actors, writers and Jungian analysts were at the party, all of them fascinated by Martha's interpretation of Greek myths. But to me she had become a distant figure again, the celebrated goddess of dance, and the love affair of the mind, that weekend on Shelter Island, seemed gone forever.

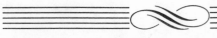

8. Composer and Librettist

Richard Wagner wrote his own libretti; Gian-Carlo Menotti writes his. There must be others but these two come to mind most prominently. To be able to imagine a dramatic situation and find both the right words and the right musical sounds for it is a rare gift; most of us have to be content with inventing just one.

Our only consolation is that purely operatic composers, even those who did not write their own libretti, were often active only in the theater and never had the pleasure of writing piano pieces, string quartets or violin concertos. Perhaps this singular concentration on theatrical composition precludes the ability to write music whose shape does not depend upon a plot. Yet in Elizabethan times composers wrote their own poems, set them to music, sang them and accompanied themselves on the lute. Some folksingers do this even today. Then there is Mozart, who excelled at opera and all the other forms as well—although he did not write his own libretti.

Those of us interested in setting text for chorus or solo voice, and in writing an occasional opera, are constantly reading poetry and plays, secretly hoping all the while to meet our ideal collaborator someday. My own reaction to poetry is instant: this is for me, this is not for me. Sometimes I even hear music the first time I read a poem. This does not mean that I instantly set it to music—it may deal with a topic I am not interested in at the time—but I do keep it in the back of my mind until the moment is ripe, sometimes years later.

What in poetry attracts the musician's ear? Not clever play with words; this would be lost in the music. Not even philosophical depth. If one needs to read a poem twice to get its meaning, one surely doesn't want to hear it sung. To my ear a poem must be strong in three elements: rhythm, imagery and meaning. In a setting for chorus a few lines will often be repeated many times, especially in contrapuntal sections, where the word is no longer understood but must be remembered. Hence rhythm is of primary importance, since it often shapes the musical idea. While verse forms based on Greek metrical schemes are too repetitive for twentieth-century sensibilities, the psalms, for example, offer rhythmic variety:

Give thanks   unto the Lord,   for His

mer - cy en - dureth   for   - ever.

In the second half of this phrase the words themselves impose a change of meter or, if you will, create an organic compilation of seven beats (four plus three).

What sort of imagery excites the musical mind? Here are some lines from Isaiah that simply cry out for music:

> *The daughters of Zion are haughty:*
> *and walk with stretched-forth necks and wanton eyes,*
> *walking and mincing as they go,*
> *and making a tinkling with their feet.*

Equally vivid is the imagery in Emily Dickinson's poem:

> *"Hope" is the thing with feathers—*
> *That perches in the soul—*
> *And sings the tune without the words—*
> *And never stops—at all—*

Meaning is the third element one looks for in poetry for choral setting, the kind of meaning that members of a chorus can identify with and will enjoy singing. The following lines come from different parts of William Blake's *The Four Zoas.* I used them in a large-scale choral work called *Images of Man:*

> *Everything that lives is holy.*

> *It is an easy thing to triumph in the summer's sun.*

What is the price of experience?
Do men buy it for a song?

Rise from the dews of death, for the Eternal Man is risen.

O Prince of Light, where art thou?

Man lives not by self alone, but in his brother's face.

When Brooklyn College asked me to write a work to commemorate its fiftieth anniversary, I decided to use only texts related to Brooklyn. Walt Whitman, who had lived and worked a good part of his life in Brooklyn, was an obvious choice, and his "Poets to Come" seemed to fit the occasion. Norman Rosten's sprightly poem "Brooklyn Bridge" made a good opening; poems by two members of the Brooklyn College faculty, John Ashbery and Susan Fromberg Schaeffer, were included; and I was granted permission by the Thomas Wolfe estate to adapt excerpts from his short story "Only the Dead Know Brooklyn," which became a macabre scherzo.

I went even further in mixing texts by different authors when I wrote *Music Is* for the Phi Mu Alpha Sinfonia fraternity. It was a short work, and almost every line was by a different author:

Music is said to be the speech of angels.

Music is the perfection of the soul.

Music is the poor man's Parnassus.

It is the fragrance of the universe.

It is the eye of the ear.

It is the least disagreeable of noises.

It is the moonlight in the gloomy night of life.

In sweet music is such art,
    Killing care and grief of heart
    Fall asleep, or hearing, die.

Music is a discipline, and a mistress of order and good manners.

It makes people more moral and more reasonable.

Music is divine and Satan is its enemy.

The devil does not stay where music is.

Without music life would be a mistake.

The first seven lines are by Thomas Carlyle, Edgar Allan Poe, Ralph Waldo Emerson, Giuseppe Mazzini, Thomas Draxe, Samuel Johnson and Jean Paul Richter respectively. The next three are from Shakespeare's *Henry VIII,* the next four by Martin Luther and the last is by Friedrich Nietzsche.

Only once did I try to write my own text. In the late fifties a number of composers were asked to contribute to the Juilliard Repertory Project, a government-sponsored effort to improve the music used in our schools. I was asked to contribute a song suitable for children in the sixth grade, and I wrote a song called "Midnight." I went back into the recesses of memory to recollect a German poem that had appealed to me in my own childhood, probably because of its play with sound and word and its juxtaposition of absurdities. I modernized its imagery somewhat and set it to music as a canon:

> *It is midnight.*
> *The sun is shining brightly*
> *And a car is racing slowly down the river.*
>
> *It is summer.*
> *Snow is falling lightly.*
> *It is warm and yet I shiver.*
>
> *I saw a rocket walk,*
> *I heard a turtle talk,*
> *I saw a dog with three legs,*
> *I saw four square eggs.*
> *Do you know, do you know why I shiver?*

When setting a poem by a living writer or one still protected by copyright, one must obtain permission. In some cases it cannot be secured, or else it involves long correspondence with publishers, sometimes so drawn-out that the initial impulse to use the poem is lost. Not always, though. E. E. Cummings was still alive when I set his poem "My Sweet Old Etcetera" to music, and when I wrote to ask for permission I was told that he wanted to see my setting of his poem; his approval depended upon his liking it. When I sent my music he liked it and asked for a single payment of five dollars.

The estate of D. H. Lawrence is neither as simple to deal with nor as cooperative. Once I asked permission to use an excerpt from Lawrence's poem "The Ship of Death." The reply was that it had to be either the whole poem or nothing, so it was nothing. On the other hand, the Carl Sandburg estate did allow me to set excerpts from *The People, Yes.*

Since choral settings require so few words, it is important to be able to excerpt. In larger works different lines from the same poem can be juxtaposed effectively or handled simultaneously in counterpoint. I have done this with lines from the book of Ecclesiastes, William Blake and his great predecessor Isaiah.

Cutting, editing and juxtaposing is clearly not the same as working with a living human being, one who can talk back, has good ideas and collaborates in many unanticipated ways to make the result truly a joint accomplishment. This becomes particularly important when setting text for solo voice or when writing for the musical theater. The composer no longer looks simply for a few significant lines that he can shape into a musical whole—just think of all the music written over the centuries on the few syllables of "Kyrie Eleison"—but demands a poem that has dramatic shape in itself. It must also have a strong mood and not be verbose, pompous or overly repetitious.

It takes longer to sing a line than it does to speak it; therefore a play has to be cut considerably before it can become an opera. Compare Shakespeare's *Othello* with Verdi's *Otello,* or Büchner's *Woyzeck* with Berg's *Wozzeck.* When I became interested in Michel de Ghelderode's *Pantagleize,* his widow kindly and wisely gave me permission to shorten his play when I turned it into a libretto.

Early in my career I did have an occasional collaborator, but none satisfactory enough to work with twice. I had pretty much resigned myself to cutting, editing and juxtaposing by myself when I met Gail Godwin at Yaddo, the artists' colony, during the summer of 1972. At that time there was no thought of collaboration; she was a writer of fiction and I of music, two totally different fields that seemed to have no point of artistic contact. Even after we decided to live together, the possibility of collaborating did not occur to either of us. I knew that Gail was extraordinarily musical, not through education but innately. She also understood the inner gestures of music. In a world where most people have been conditioned to ignore the music that surrounds them, she retained an awareness of sound that astonished me. Though she claimed never to listen to me while I worked behind the closed doors of my studio, she always recognized what I was playing and would say that it reminded her of some other work I had written. Invariably she would be right. (While it is irrelevant in this context, readers of Gail's fiction know how large a part music plays in her books.)

About three years after our decision to live together, Gail and I were walking up one of the hills near our house in upstate New York while I complained bitterly about the insensitivity of a librettist who was sending me uninspired pages of dialogue and overly wordy, unmusical pages for a commission that I had accepted. As I ranted, it suddenly struck me that I lived with a highly musical writer, yet had never even thought of the possibility of collaborating with her.

Gail had just written a short story in which there was reference to a Saint Pelagia, a fourth-century woman of pleasure who had given up her kind of life to become not just a nun but a monk. In the short story, Pelagia's fate was not of primary importance, but I thought it could be the main plot in a modern operatic handling with elements of the old miracle play, the *Sacra Rappresentazione*. Apparently there were several versions of the legend of Pelagia, differing mostly in what happened to her after she became a monk, and since that afternoon there is one more: Gail's.

As we continued to talk, the story began to take shape, as did the way to treat it. I had never in my life been so close to creating drama and words. We decided that since

Working with Gail Godwin
© 1986 THOMAS VICTOR

we had only three singers at our disposal, Pelagia would play herself and "Pelagius," the monk, and that the soprano and baritone could, with quick costume changes, each play more than one person. The five musicians would be on stage and be involved in the action. Gail thought of a number of ways of doing this, and when we came home from our walk she went straight to her study. A few hours later she handed me the opening scene of what was to be called *The Last Lover*.

Pelagia enters with her maid, surrounded by the musicians, who play as they walk in, and sings a sort of "catalogue duet" (she *is* a female Don Giovanni) with the maid. One of the musicians reminds Pelagia of a man in her past. She and the maid try to remember who it was: "Attractus? Severinus? Braga, the Black? Finian, the Younger, or his brother, the Older? Little Nonnatus or Blandinus, the Bore? . . . So many, ah, so many."

It did not take me long to put this to music, and a few days later we discussed the next scene, Pelagia's meeting the Holy Man, who impresses her with his sincerity, devotion and resistance to her flirtatious advances. Afterward Gail again went to her study and soon handed me the scene.

Thus we went on to the Seducer (the Devil), sung by the same baritone who had been the Holy Man, who asks Pelagia to try various dances with him. She rejects his proposals, and there is a duet in which both pursue their own thoughts. After he leaves, she decides, in a lovely

Joanna Simon and Linda Phillips at the premiere of The Last Lover

monologue, which became an aria the same afternoon, to change her ways and become a monk. As she sings, she disposes of her ostentatious jewelry piece by piece, and at the end, when she says she will "obliterate every last shadow of my former self," one of the musicians helps her put on a monk's robe and hood.

Gail invented the young nun who falls in love with Brother Pelagius (a duet for two female voices), and who is made pregnant by the Seducer. She also employed the musicians in the action brilliantly by having them ask questions, both serious and sarcastic, after the trial, in which Pelagius remains silent and does not answer the accusation that she has seduced the young nun. A judge pronounces sentence: Pelagius is to be banished for life.

In the final scene the flute player, the same one who reminded Pelagia of a former lover in the opening scene, walks up to the dead Pelagius while playing a piccolo, and dramatically removes "his" hood so the audience can see her long, blond hair. The Seducer sings a philosophical, sardonic epilogue, and then the musicians leave one by one, having played their individual farewells to Pelagia.

Later Gail said that she thought the operatic setting of Pelagia's story was more effective than the narrative one and that she had never been totally satisfied with her short story. She also said that she felt quite uninhibited writing those pages "because nobody ever remembers the librettist anyway," and that she did not mind leaving the final choice of words to me. Thus, by writing more text than I needed, she gave me the opportunity to choose words and match their rhythm to musical rhythm. And if I needed another syllable, an extra line or a more singable word in a certain bar, I could simply knock on her creative door and it would be forthcoming—something I could not do with William Blake, Isaiah or whoever wrote the book of Ecclesiastes.

Going to rehearsals of *The Last Lover* with Gail—the work had its premiere at the Caramoor Festival—was also a new experience. I like singers to look their part, but I leave sets, costumes and other visual aspects of a production to the experts in those fields. Not Gail. She was deeply interested in every facet of the interpretation of her characters, and our excellent cast often consulted her on the way to give proper meaning and intonation to her lines. What they wore and how they behaved in their surroundings also mattered much to her, while I was more concerned with how they sang.

There have been a number of other productions of *The Last Lover* since, in churches, concert halls and chamber-opera houses; most of them were in costume, a few in evening clothes and one with a cast wearing masks, and all of them were more different from one another than any purely musical interpretations ever are.

When I was asked to compose a work for William Steinberg's farewell concert as music director of the Pittsburgh Symphony, I again turned to Gail. Seymour Rosen, the

manager of the orchestra, had told me that the second part
of the program would be Beethoven's Ninth—a difficult act
to precede, to turn a stage cliché around—and that I could
use up to four soloists, a chorus and the orchestra. I had
written much for chorus but little for solo voice and nothing at all for solo voice and orchestra. Gail suggested that
we write something personal for the occasion, perhaps the
autobiographical notes of a musician, in honor of Steinberg's life as a maker of music. I liked the idea, and the work
that eventually emerged was called *Journals of a Songmaker.*
The title was Gail's, as was the idea of having it consist of
entries in a journal.

To start she asked me to write some entries in an imagined journal myself, perhaps a passage that dealt with the
genesis of a musical idea. The only time in my life I had
kept a journal was during my first sojourn in the Western
Desert of North Africa. At the time I was nineteen years old
and was in a truck convoy from Cairo to Tobruk, a much-
fought-over town in Libya that was then in our hands. It
was the first time I had slept under a truck in a heavy rain
—I had no idea it could rain so heavily in the desert—or
had seen a burned-out German tank and a totally demol-
ished city, and all these became entries in my journal, a little
notebook that I carried in my back pocket. After a few days
I realized that there was really nothing extraordinary in my
experiences or observations, so I turned the journal into an
address book, keeping the names and home addresses of

soldier-friends for years—without, of course, ever contacting a single one of them after the war.

Now, many years later, I sat with a pad and pencil, trying to describe in words how a musical idea originates. Once I had been asked a similar question by Robert Sherman during an interview on the radio station of the *New York Times.* I answered truthfully that my first impulse is often rhythmic and that only later do I shape the initial rhythmic idea melodically. Sherman, who had asked this question of a number of composers, told me some of their replies.

All this was of no help to me now. Gail was going to write a poetic text and I had to give her some basic information. Suddenly I heard sounds, high sounds made by harmonics on the violin, trills in the high woodwinds, and running passages on the harp, vibraphone and piano. I could write these sounds down in musical notation, but to describe them? Finally I scribbled down a few words and gave them to Gail.

In the final version of *Journals of a Songmaker* the orchestra begins with the very sounds I heard that day. Then the baritone comes in and sings:

> *Sound. Sounds. Tinkly. Fragile. Frightening.*
> *Babbling, burbling, purling, trilling.*
> *Baying, bleating . . . pandemonium.*
>
> *Sounds. That is my life. That is how it is.*

I could not have written these lines, nor the next ones. I did give Gail some notes for them, but the words are hers. The baritone continues:

> *How many sounds are there in all, I wonder?*
> *I don't need to know. I need to hear sounds,*
>   *to shape them, stretch them, shrink them,*
>   *tear them apart, prune them and mix them,*
>   *bring out their best and their worst,*
>   *bend them to my will.*
> *Do I bend them, or do they bend me?*
> *I don't need to know. I am not a philosopher.*
> *I am a musician.*
> *Why does a musician keep a journal?*
> *His province is sound, not words.*
> *A journal makes one self-conscious.*
> *Like listening to oneself think.*
> *Like listening to oneself listening to oneself think.*
> *I fall asleep with sounds,*
> *And when I wake—or when they wake me—*
> *I must tend to them.*

These lines describe a composer's life—or at least they describe mine. (Once I told a psychiatrist sitting next to me at a dinner party that I dream music almost every night, and in return he gave me an incredulous look. Probably not one of his patients had ever said this.)

Our baritone, whom Gail had called a Songmaker, a word I liked, next sings that his first memory is of a woman's voice. The image appealed to me and, being a songmaker, I wanted to hear her voice, a tender, wordless chant. We decided to add a soprano to our score; she could also represent other women in our musician's life.

After a few brief journal entries sung by the baritone, the soprano returns as Delfina, a singer who has sung our musician's songs and has also been his lover. In the brief scene Gail wrote for them, he hands her a new song and also tells her that they must part as lovers:

> *Why does my art parallel my life?*
> *Or do I orchestrate my life to fit my art?*

She is a proud woman. Her final words to him are:

> *You were never good at endings.*

Our baritone has a bad night, drinks himself to sleep and is haunted by frightening visions and images. This is accompanied by dramatic, macabre music in 5/8 time, which Steinberg conducted with great force:

> *What an interminable dusk my life seems.*
> *Why bother to go on?*
> *Why not stop the clock altogether?*
>
> *I hate the sounds I make.*
> *They set my teeth on edge.*

Howl, vile creatures of the night!
Howl and drown my monotonous rage!

In his moment of despair the Songmaker turns to Bach, as I myself often have. He brings order into one's life and lets one see things in their proper perspective. When we came to that moment in the piece, I composed a Bach-like snatch of music for the piano (performed, as it happened, by the same young woman who had been so angered by my playing the piano rehearsal). There was a deep hush in the hall when she did so. Then the baritone sings, "Thank God for Bach," and a long chuckle rose from the audience.

There was a third woman in our musician's life, a young woman named Marianne Clare, who writes him a letter. In it she says:

Dear Sir—Maestro: Please forgive my boldness. This evening I am in a daring mood. I played your music. It convinces me that all the passionate things in the world are not dead. They only slumber from time to time.

She asks his advice:

I hear sounds in my head. Noble sounds that contain the entire emotion I wish to express. But when I hurry to write them down, something gets lost. It is not quite so noble. It is a little like when I was a child at the seashore. I would try to carry the ocean in my hands. Some always got lost before I reached my castle. How do you make the reality live up to your dreams?

The musician decides to answer her, and the prospect elates him:

> *Why is it I feel such anticipation?*
> *Why is it I feel a certain lightness when I think*
> *of all I am going to tell her*
> *When I write this afternoon?*
> *What is this strange lightness,*
> *This feeling of limitless freedom?*
> *This feeling of unbounded, limitless freedom?*

Collaborating with Gail on this work brought me closer to understanding the relationship of what Goethe called *Dichtung und Wahrheit,* which can be translated as "poetic invention and truth," something that has always puzzled the layman when he studies the imaginative writer. How does something "true" change into something "poetically invented"? Too much has already been said on this topic for me to add anything significant. Let me say only that it is a wonderful process, as wonderful as thinking up music, which is the highest compliment a musician can pay.

In the late seventies the National Opera Institute in Washington had the idea that a modern opera should have a chance to try out, just as every Broadway show does, and gave grants for this purpose. Gail and I were interested in the proposition, and so was the Minnesota Opera Company, an active, open-to-new-ideas organization. As a result, we flew to Minneapolis often one winter to collaborate on an opera called *Apollonia,* which was to be a mixture of the realistic and the fantastical. Apollonia had the powers to make people become what they wanted to be, and whenever she employed these powers I used an electric organ. We plotted the opera and I wrote the music as we went along, trying out each scene with members of the Minnesota company. I saw many advantages in this procedure, but also some drawbacks. To be able to try out a theatrical idea with real singers and then discard it if it does not work, or else change it until it does, is an opportunity not normally offered a composer and librettist. On the other hand, the composer and librettist lose momentum and the integrity of their original concept by listening to too many people's ideas, suggestions, critical comments and proposals for improvement.

Our next collaboration, *Anna Margarita's Will,* had a different beginning: I actually wrote the opening lines myself. It happened in an unexpected way. The writer James Purdy, a neighbor in Brooklyn Heights, where I have an apartment, was giving a course on the short story that was offered on Tuesday evenings. Since I was free at that time, I signed up for it because I thought it would be interesting. It was. At first Purdy discussed short stories by well-known writers, but one evening he said, "I would like you to try your hand at a short story yourselves. Begin by writing a paragraph that is spoken by a person as different from yourself as you can imagine, and let me see it next week."

Later that evening I had an image of a woman, still young, contemplating death and deciding to make her will. Her name leaped into my mind, and I wrote: "I, Anna Margarita Wells, of seventeen Schoonmaker Lane, hereby make my will and testament. I am not about to die. I am not even old yet, I am, as they say, of sound body and mind. I don't have children, nor brothers and sisters."

Still later that night I set these lines to music for a soprano voice and a few instruments. I never showed the lines to James Purdy, but I did give them to Gail when I came home. She liked this kernel, and we decided to make the words the beginning of a dramatic monologue. Gail continued the opening paragraph:

And since I do have property, some acquired and much inherited, I am troubled by the thought that it would all go to my Cousin Loulie in Alabama, who does not need it, and would feel more inconvenienced than grateful.

After an instrumental interlude, Anna Margarita sings:

Often lately, at the sunset hour, I look out at the hills tinctured orange with the fading light and I call up the people in my life to whom I would like to leave something of myself, people who have given me what can never be returned.

She remembers her mother, who left her a box of photographs and a diary written in purple ink; her father, who taught her to ride and gave her courage and nerve; Sister Ursula, who sat by her bed the night her father died.

Each of these characters turned into a song or section of the dramatic monologue that was different in character and mood. Anna Margarita evokes each one in turn, as she tries to find someone suitable to inherit her wealth. Then she remembers Rudy, a married lover (his wife would open the letter and ask, "Who is this Anna Margarita Wells?"), and Franklin, her tragic college love, whose advice to her had been: "Drink deep, Anna Margarita, drink deep, or don't drink at all." Franklin had "drunk so deep he reached the bottom of the well." He had gone to the corner bar, bought everyone a drink, announced: "Time, gentlemen, time," and shot himself.

Anna Margarita finds it easy to make small bequests, but the bulk will still go to cousin Loulie. Then we hear Loulie's entertaining reaction to inheriting Anna's estate, which I set in a slightly jazzy way.

> *Oh, Lordie, look what Cousin Anna's done.*
> *She's left me her estate.*
> *What good to me are houses in the North,*
> *With all that snow and all that crime?*

> *I'm touched, of course, but really,*
> *That emerald necklace would have been enough.*

In a sense Anna becomes all those people of whom she speaks. In the end she decides that all is not over and sings: "I will go down to the stream and plant a willow tree, in hopes of all that still might be, so I can watch it grow while I live."

Not everything for voice I have done in recent years has been in collaboration with Gail. In 1985 I was asked to appear at several concerts with a young string quartet that gives concerts for audiences of senior citizens, and they played a string quartet I had written at the age of twenty-three. Afterward I spoke to the audience and answered their questions, which led to some interesting exchanges. This juxtaposition of young and old made me curious about what poets have said on this subject. There is a great deal, of course, and the eventual result was a song cycle I called *Songs of Youth and Age.* It opens with Walt Whitman's "Youth, large lusty, loving—youth full of grace, force, fascination,/Do you know that Old Age may come after you with equal grace, force, fascination?" Charles Kingsley's "Young and Old" follows, a metrically strong poem with a folksy quality. His advice to the old is to "creep home and look for a face you loved when all was young." The third song is based on a medieval poem: "The life of this world is governed by wind, weeping, darkness and pangs." For a positive conclusion I chose the famous lines from Tennyson's "Ulysses" beginning "Old age hath yet his honour and his toil" and ending "to strive, to seek, to find, and not to yield."

Though I enjoyed this project, it was very different from the actual plotting and shaping of characters and situations when working with Gail. All my life I had listened for sounds within myself, until she made me listen for words when she asked me to write the opening page of *Journals of a Songmaker*. If I had not written *that* page, I might never have written *these* pages.

9. Audiences

When David Bar-Illan played my third piano concerto
with the American Symphony Orchestra at Carnegie Hall
on January 6, 1980, the man who sat next to me rose and
walked out of the hall as soon as the first chord was struck.
I did not run after him to ask him why he had not even
waited for the second chord before making such a drastic
decision; but I did follow him with my eyes through the
exit door, which a young usher, also staring at him, held
open for him.

I have thought about that man often since. Let us call him
Mr. X.

My first reaction to his act was anger. Was he not being
rude to stalk out like that, showing his disdain for the
composer, as well as his contempt for those who stayed to
listen? Admittedly my third piano concerto does begin with
a loud, provocatively harsh chord. Was I subconsciously
following Richard Strauss's advice to start a piece with a
bang ("Just wake them up; after that you can do whatever
you want," he is supposed to have said), rather than beginning gently, as is my natural inclination?

Going over the score of my second piano concerto with David Bar-Illan

Did the dissonance of my first chord so frighten Mr. X that he could tolerate no more? I can't believe this. Any horror movie has more dissonance in it than my first chord. Was he perhaps one of those who was only interested in *who* was playing and not in *what* was being played? Concert announcements often try to lure audiences to hear famous performers without telling them what is on the program. People one meets on airplanes, or in similar casual situations, will often say: "I went to hear"—many of them will say "see"—"Arrau," or "Menuhin," or "Serkin." When you ask, "What did he play?" they usually do not remember.

Mr. X had heard or read about my concert. Perhaps he was a fan of Bar-Illan's and went to all his performances without looking at the details of the program. He had dressed and walked or driven to the concert and had sat quietly through the overture preceding my piece. Then, probably hoping that the next piece would be by Liszt, Mr. X had looked at the program and seen that the concerto was by someone named Starer. He probably skimmed my biography printed in the program, then folded his hands patiently in his lap, anticipating the worst. My first chord confirmed his fears, his body rebelled and he got up and left.

Am I trying to understand Mr. X? I will and I must. We modern composers do have a bad reputation, some of it quite deserved. A great deal of unmitigated ugliness has been served to audiences, and not much that gives pleasure or even food for thought. It is easy to blame the audience.

Some years ago Milton Babbitt wrote a much-quoted article called "Who Cares If You Listen?" Clearly he does not care, and very few indeed do listen.

Who is at fault? *What* is at fault? No one will deny that there has to be experimentation; without it there can be no progress. But does every musical experiment have to be exposed to the public? Medical experiments are carried out over long periods of time, and only when the results are proven to be successful are they offered to the wide public. We even have government departments that have to certify the validity of a new treatment or drug before it can be used or bought.

Who is to make such decisions in music? There is a modern music establishment, which runs concert series, gives prizes and controls the committees that dispense grants. Unfortunately this establishment is run by the very people whose music has driven audiences away from concerts of new music. They are the ones who write articles like "Who Cares If You Listen?"

Then should *critics* decide which musical experiment is to be offered to the public? In the days when the bourgeoisie could still be shocked—and when it was still fun to shock it—critics saw their role as defenders of values; they had to protect the bourgeoisie from the aggression of daring sound-makers. We have all read about the negative critical reaction that Beethoven encountered (he was called "reckless and unintelligible"), and Chopin was harshly criticized for his unexpected harmonic turns, which broke unwritten rules. The celebrated premiere of Stravinsky's *Rite of Spring* produced shouts and even fistfights among those present. But today, when concert audiences are asked to listen to a single note for two hours, or to unintelligible sounds coming out of four different loudspeakers, or even to make sounds themselves, most critics no longer see themselves as defenders of a sacred past. Many of them look primarily for the new, for that which will demand and perhaps get attention, for anything that still might be termed sensational. If it still exists at all, the bourgeoisie has long ceased being shocked.

Why did Mr. X leave so suddenly? In a way I admire him for doing so. Too many people will sit through almost anything and tolerate it; at least he had convictions and acted according to them. Is he important? Yes, he is. In the long run audiences do determine which music survives and which does not. No performer will persist in playing what his listeners truly hate, even if the press adores it. In the long run instrumentalists and conductors will play only what people are willing to hear more than once, music that gains upon repetition, music that has depths that need to be explored. Many pieces of music have sensational premieres and then within a few years fade from the repertory; others enter the world quietly but establish themselves firmly in the minds of music lovers, who want to hear them again and again.

The *Rite of Spring* has led a fairly normal life for a piece of "new" art: it shocked its initial hearers, soon became accepted and was eventually considered a masterpiece. Nowadays there is hardly a movie in which one does not hear an imitation of it, and surely Mr. X wouldn't walk out of a performance of it. Schönberg's *Pierrot Lunaire,* on the other hand, also written just before World War I, was played as recently as 1981 at Tanglewood in a "contemporary music festival." Surely that is an indication of something abnormal.

Do these festivals of contemporary or quasi-contemporary music really help the cause of new music? I wonder. It seems to me that they have created an artistic ghetto, which is visited by only a tiny fraction of the music-loving population. The diet shelf in a bookstore is full of books telling you to eat only proteins or only carbohydrates. But sensible doctors advise that it is better to eat just a little less of everything. By the same token the ideal musical menu includes a variety of styles, because if art is to continue as a living element, it must contain something new, or at least something of its own time. The modern music festivals have, I think, contributed much to the alienation of the larger audience.

There are not only many kinds of music; there are also many different kinds of audiences. Some *listen* to music; some ignore it. Much music is intended to be ignored, or to serve subconsciously the aims of those who supply it. Music at supermarkets—millions are exposed to it every day, whether they want to be or not—determines the speed with which shoppers push their carts. Once I saw a woman dance to the music in a supermarket. Everyone made a wide, embarrassed circle around her; her crime had been to respond to music which it is only proper to ignore. Have you ever known anyone not to get off an elevator just to hear the rest of the piece that was being played?

Music to be ignored has had several devastating effects. It has produced an entire generation that does not know how to listen to music but uses it as an ever-present background to their conversation, studies or other activities. It has also reduced music of high intellectual, emotional and moral value to the same level.

The other day at a friend's house we sat down to dinner as the opening movement of a late Beethoven quartet came out of the elegant speakers. My hosts were not rednecks; they were people who read intelligent books, magazines and papers, who go to the theater and to museums. The quality of the sound was superb, better than any live string quartet in the next room could have produced. But instead of the next record descending at the end of the first, the needle simply went back to the beginning, so that by the time dessert was served, we had heard the first movement five times. I had reached the limits of my patience, and asked quietly, "Could we please hear the second movement of the

Beethoven?" The host, embarrassed, got up, apologized and fixed the record player.

What troubled me most was that no one else at the table —it was a large party of highly cultured people—had noticed. Beethoven had indeed become "elevator" music. I knew it was gauche of me to mention it, but how many times can you listen to the same music over and over, no matter how good the dinner is? There is music suitable for funerals, for military parades, for parties and for dining, but the late Beethoven quartets were not meant to be heard above the sounds of knives, forks and light chatter.

A musician friend told me that whenever he goes to his accountant to do his income tax, the man quickly switches to Mozart. "I can listen either to you or to Mozart," my friend finally told him, "but I cannot listen to both of you at the same time."

When I speak of listeners, I mean people who are giving their full attention to the music, not those who notice it only when it is loud enough, or those who, aided by chemicals, enjoy listening to five notes being mindlessly repeated, nor even all those who dream their dreams to the sound of music and are perhaps gently influenced by it (as the music gets louder they decide to tell their bosses what they really think of them; as it becomes softer they think they'd better not) but are not giving it their full attention.

Major orchestras in major cities give concerts on Friday

afternoon, and it is said of them that the applause can't be heard because the ladies never take their gloves off. This is an unkind joke, but the ladies do leave at a quarter past four, whether the concert is over or not, in order to get to their bridge parties or to catch their trains back to suburbia. Yet these same ladies are among the main supporters of our orchestras.

Mr. X does not belong to any of those groups slightly caricatured by me. Let me start with what I sense about him: He has a genuine need for music, even a hunger for it, and would consider his life impoverished without it. My first encounter with people of this sort who seem to draw moral strength from music happened many years ago.

My sister joined a kibbutz in Palestine in the early forties. In those days volunteers to these settlements lived their idealism to the fullest; they worked the land to make it fruitful again and avoided all the "Jewish" professions— law, medicine and business. The women also lived their feminism to the fullest; they did hard physical labor and carried arms. When they first set out to cultivate land that had been neglected for centuries, they lived in tents. They had only one building with a roof, a wooden shed in which they ate, held their meetings and spent their social evenings. There was an upright piano in that building, and every time I visited my sister's kibbutz I played for its members. They were always tired, and a few of them carried rifles when they came in to listen. They wanted only the most serious

music, Bach and Beethoven especially, but they looked
younger and less tired when they left those impromptu
concerts. It was tremendously satisfying to see their faces
changed by the music.

During my military service I spent a pleasant year in
Cairo. There was a place there called Music for All, which
had a concert most afternoons and every evening. Local
musicians played, as well as Allied soldiers, and if there was
no live music to be had, the audience listened to recordings.
Cairo was full of foreigners in 1944: troops in British,
Australian, New Zealand, South African and American uniforms; refugees from most European countries; and the
regular residents—Syrians, Greeks, Lebanese and what used
to be called Levantine, mixtures of various ingredients.
There were also young Egyptian intellectuals with leanings
to classical music. What brought all these disparate people
together in the afternoon or evening? Obviously it was the
music. After the concerts they drank tea, ate pastries and
made friends. They would never have talked to each other
without Music for All.

New York has many audiences. There is one for every
kind of music, from that which sells out Madison Square
Garden in two hours to that which attracts seven people,
five of them relatives of the performer. Choral concerts,
ancient music concerts, jazz, ethnic and computer music
concerts—each of them draws its own admirers. Some audiences are so specialized that they want to hear only their

particular kind of music. Lovers of nineteenth-century opera, for example, when faced with a new opera in their subscription series, would probably rather give their ticket to a neighbor than hear the new work. (Management sees to it that they do not have to make this decision often.) Yet we read how each new opera by Verdi, each new symphonic poem by Strauss, was eagerly awaited by its audience. Even Stravinsky's changes in style and direction and Koussevitzky's new American composers were fully accepted. What has happened since? What have we done to drive Mr. X away?

In a fantasy the other night I decided to speak to Mr. X. For some reason our conversation took place in the old Carnegie Tavern. It does not exist anymore, but it was behind Carnegie Hall, and many people went there after concerts, as did members of the New York Philharmonic. Occasionally people like Mitropoulos would walk in for a drink. In my youth I once even saw Bruno Walter there.

The old Carnegie Tavern was a comfortable place. It had wooden chairs and tables and waiters in frayed dress coats and ready-made bow ties, with a slightly soiled white towel on their left arm with which they cleaned the table before serving you your beer. It was the sort of place where you could easily strike up a conversation with someone at the next table, especially after a concert.

In my fantasy Mr. X sat alone at a table, a glass of dark

beer before him. Sitting at the next table, I casually asked him, "How did you like the concert?"

"I liked everything except the new piece."

"The one just before intermission?"

"Yes. When I heard the opening chord, I decided it wasn't for me, so I got up and went out to look at the posters in the lobby."

"Do you do that often?"

"Always. I'm fed up with all this new stuff and won't listen to any more of it."

I saw a chance to gain Mr. X's confidence by agreeing with him, at least partially. "A lot of bad music has been written in every era," I began. "I once went to a concert in Rome where they played only music by former choir-masters of the Sistine Chapel. Most of it was dull, uninspired and predictable, but it taught me a lesson: bad music was also written in the sixteenth, seventeenth and eighteenth centuries. We just don't play it anymore."

"Interesting," conceded Mr. X.

"There was one piece by Palestrina on the program, and it shone like a sunbeam on a cloudy day," I continued. "Did you ever notice that there are many inferior paintings in museums all over the world, and many second-rate books in libraries? Yet in music only the very best survives, it seems to me."

"You have a point."

"Even record companies, who are trying desperately

these days to find good music from earlier periods, haven't dug up much. Yet what they are doing is to be applauded. If Mendelssohn hadn't rediscovered Bach, we might have had to live without him."

It was easy for Mr. X to agree with this also, so I decided to attempt a frontal attack. "What is it you dislike so much about the music of our day?"

"Do you really want to know what I think?" he asked. "Okay, I'll tell you. They've done away with melody and rhythm and have substituted noise and sound effects."

"Surely not all of them?"

"No, but most of them."

Suddenly Mr. X became quite eloquent. Sentences spewed out of him as though he had formulated them over a long period of time and was just waiting for an occasion to say them.

"I divide them into several kinds," he said. "First, there is the School of Meaningless Sounds, as I call it. The music gesticulates wildly, but there is no discernible melody or rhythm in it. At first I thought such composers were speaking a language that I didn't know. Later I discovered they were simply stringing meaningless syllables together; whether this followed a mathematical formula of twelve or some other predetermined number made no difference to me as a listener. I searched for meaning and found none."

"And whom do you include in this school?"

"Oh, Roger Sessions, Elliott Carter, Wuorinen—people

like that. Then there's the school that makes you listen to sound effects all evening. In the theater the equivalent would be actors saying *sh-sh-sh-sh, tskt-tskt-tskt* or *oo-hoo-hoo-hoo* all night long. No one would stand for that in the theater; why, then, in music? To cover up their emptiness they make the musicians walk around or wear masks or silly clothes. Do they really think that this is theatrical?"

"I suppose you mean Crumb or Druckman?"

"Yes," Mr. X said, "those two and their imitators. Another group I like to call Philosophers of Noise and Nonsense—that is, John Cage and his followers. They want to prove that noise is music—the crash cymbals in a Turkish march by Mozart are the usual example in their argument —but I'd still rather listen to music than to their noise.

"Then there are the so-called Minimalists. Minimal music for minimal minds. I simply don't have the patience to listen to them; they tell me nothing."

"But Glass and Reich have brought the audience back, haven't they?"

"The wrong kind of audience," he said angrily. "People who surround themselves with a cushion of sound and think of other things. When I listen to Bach, Mozart, Beethoven or Prokofiev, I follow their thoughts through all their changes and variations. That's what I look for in music."

"Is there no one around today who still has musical ideas, develops them and presents them in a way that interests you?"

"Perhaps," Mr. X said, "but I've stopped listening or looking for them."

Have we really lost the intelligent listener by feeding him music that has none of the values he is looking for? Are these values universal in the sense that they exist in other cultures, or did music for a discerning audience really exist in the West only for a few hundred years?

If you have reached this far in my book, dear reader (as the author might have addressed you in the last century), you clearly care about music and its future. Do you think Mr. X is right or wrong? Do you agree with him on some points but not on others? Perhaps you know Mr. X and have spoken or argued with him. Perhaps you *are* Mr. X and have walked out of a concert when you disliked the music. (I have done it myself, though never after just one chord.) If you care about music, as I think you do, you surely have opinions.

As for myself, I think we must win back Mr. X. Can we? I hope so. We can regain him by giving him music that is not tedious; music that holds his interest because of its beauty and logic; music interesting enough to demand and hold his full attention; music that—let us not be afraid to say it—gives him pleasure.

As he said, Mr. X likes to use his intelligence when he follows a composer's thoughts. He recognizes the recurrence of themes, he is aware of their being reorchestrated, he recognizes musical variation when it is presented to him. He follows the sequences of musical development; he perceives modulation and the harmonic and contrapuntal treatment of themes. He likes music of some complexity and depth, which gains upon repeated hearing not because the music has changed, but because the listener himself has developed and notices details that escaped him unsavored the last time he heard the piece.

What shall we ask of Mr. X in return? That he not form an opinion after a single chord; that he try to see what is being attempted; that he be willing to take a step into unfamiliar land.

If Mr. X ever sits next to me again at a concert and tries to leave after the first chord, I will catch him gently by the sleeve and ask, "Is it really *that* bad? Does it not deserve a chance to be heard?" And then, "What sort of future can we have, Mr. X, if we listen only to the past?"

10. Scriabin

THERE are two people in these pages whom I never knew personally: Mr. X and Scriabin. You may think that Scriabin had a profound influence on me as a composer and thus deserves a chapter. Not so, but his second piano sonata, the one in G-sharp minor, changed the course of my life. It was while playing the first movement of this sonata in a student recital that my memory failed me. Instead of continuing into the recapitulation at the end of the development section, I kept returning to the exposition and repeating it. After I had done this several times, I saw myself condemned to repeating it forever unless something drastic was done. With the courage of despair I improvised an ending in the style of Scriabin and left the stage.

To my surprise only one person noticed: my teacher. No matter; Scriabin is not terribly well known and my little bit of fakery must have been carried out with enough conviction to fool the rest of the audience. It did change the course of my life profoundly, though, because I decided that evening not only that the life of the solo pianist was not for me, but that I could never trust my memory again, ever.

Scriabin, of course, has become the symbol of those decisions.

Memory—musical memory in particular—has interested me greatly since my Scriabin debacle. I have looked into many books that deal with it, from the kind that tell you how to remember the name of every person you are introduced to at a party, to the more professional kind with unappetizing-looking pictures of the sections of the brain that deal with memory, short-term and long-term. In musical memory, of course, there are elements with which none of these books deal: stage fright and all that goes with it; finger memory, which I have never seen explained satisfactorily; and musical retention, which is by nature different from the retention of facts.

I know that the ability to memorize can be trained and developed. Perhaps this process was slightly damaged for me by the gymnasium to which I went in Vienna, whose teachers used memorizing as a punishment. For minor infractions of the Austrian behavioral code you had to memorize the opening paragraphs of Caesar's boring description of his victories in the Gallic Wars. I had to do this several times, and "Gallia est omnis divisa in partes tres" will stay with me to the grave. After committing a particularly unpardonable prank I once had to memorize the section in which Caesar describes in considerable detail the building of a bridge over the Rhine, a section studded with technical terms never encountered again, in Ovid or any of the other more readable Latin authors. Every few weeks we also had vocabulary tests for which one had to remember up to five hundred words (*Vokabeln,* as they were called), which we would never need to know again. To succeed in those classes one had to develop an effective *short*-term memory, but one also developed a resistance to the whole process.

Schoolboys in England are subjected to much memorization, but not as a punishment, which explains their different attitude toward it. Poetry in English is probably the world's most beautiful, and I have always envied British schoolboys the years they spent memorizing it, just as I have often marveled at the educated Englishman's ability to recite long poems in their entirety and complete sections from Shakespeare's plays. My own acquaintance with the English language did not begin until I was in my late teens.

To be equally at home in three or more languages has its advantages and disadvantages; sometimes the right word comes to mind, but in the wrong language. While I now think, speak, write and dream only in English, those other languages always lurk there, ready and waiting to be used. When I meet a Viennese at a cocktail party, especially someone who grew up there when I did, and we have retreated to some quiet corner, our conversation will bring back bits of dialect that I have not thought of in years. When I visit Israel, I try to pick up currently fashionable slang, and by mixing it into my Hebrew, I can still pass for a native. Even languages that I do not know well have a way of returning when needed. After two or three days in France I think and dream in French. To enjoy this schizophrenia, one must truly love languages and the differences between people that they reveal.

French was the first foreign language I was taught, by the same governess who discovered my absolute pitch. Austrians do not share the Germans' hatred of all things French —after all, Marie Antoinette was Austrian—and it was considered chic to mix French expressions, often quite Austrianized, into one's daily language. *Antichambrieren*—waiting in the lobby—is one of my favorites of that genre.

Next came Latin and Greek, taught at the gymnasium. My foreign language in Jerusalem was Arabic, of which I have retained little, but still enough to understand conversations between waiters in Middle Eastern restaurants. English came in my late teens, and was solidified by my three years' service with British forces. In my forties I spent a year in Rome. I decided that I did not want to live like a foreigner, took Italian lessons daily from a lovely professoressa in an elegant palazzo, and discovered that in such favorable circumstances it was still possible to acquire a new language, even at the age of forty. The first time I used the subjunctive I felt almost accepted by Italian society; still, if I don't keep it up, my Italian disappears.

Knowing a language and not showing it gives you a wonderful chance to eavesdrop or even to spy. To be the victim of this is a shock. In 1943, my first year of military

service, after the Cyrenaica and Libya had been finally taken
from the Germans, the British ran a troop train from Cairo
to Tobruk. The ride could take anywhere from two days
to a week, depending upon weather conditions—a sand-
storm might cover the single track—and activity by the
Luftwaffe. The air was always full of sand and the coaches
smelled of too many men who had not washed for a while.
On the trip I sat next to another soldier from Palestine and
we talked quietly to each other in Hebrew. Opposite us sat
a handsome Nordic type: high cheekboned, blond and with
no body hair (our uniform was shorts and short-sleeved
shirts). When they were open, his eyes were a piercing blue.

Since we were conversing in Hebrew, my friend from
Palestine and I felt free to talk about anything, and he felt
that the Nordic type opposite might be Slavic. We specu-
lated for some time while the man continued to sleep.

At dawn the train stopped at a desert camp and we got
off to get our rations for the day: a can of bully beef (canned
corned beef from Argentina), a tin of herring in tomato
sauce, crackers and, most precious, a bottle of brown, brack-
ish but drinkable water. Then we reboarded for another
long day and a night. The man opposite us seemed immersed
in a book; we tried to talk to him, but he barely answered
our direct questions. "Typical Englishman," my friend
commented loudly in Hebrew. "He won't talk to us until
we've been properly introduced." The next morning, when
the train finally arrived in Tobruk and we were about to

disperse to our different units, he finally addressed us and said with a broad smile, in fluent, accent-free Hebrew, "Have a nice time. I enjoyed listening to you."

Some months later when I met this man again in Cairo we had a drink together. He told me that he was Polish, had been a student at the Hebrew University when the war broke out and had enlisted in the British forces. Now he was working for intelligence and had the pleasant job of taking captured senior German officers to the nightclubs of Cairo because, when drunk, they were more likely to give information than when formally questioned. After the war he became well known under the stage name Chan Canasta, doing mind-reading and sophisticated card tricks in theaters in England and the United States. We became friends, and I have since done unto others what he did unto me, though never for thirty-six hours.

Is the ability to retain another language an accomplishment of memory? I believe so. If I have a memory for language, why not for music? If I can remember Viennese slang, why not Scriabin's second piano sonata?

I have spoken to many musical performers about their memory, and some of them truly amaze me. There are singers who can perform fifteen or more operatic parts in various languages at short notice. Many violinists and pianists offer conductors and managers lists of repertory consisting of up to twenty concerti. (This is in addition to several recital programs they offer to potential arrangers of programs for concert series. If one pianist has just played the "Appassionata" in a certain town, the next pianist will have to play something else.)

I have asked many performers how they do it, and the answer I usually get is that it is easy. Many pianists have told me that they never have to consciously memorize; they say that as they learn a piece—"study" might be a better word —it commits itself to their memory and stays there indelibly. Since I have seen them do it, I must believe that what they say is true. Such performers also speak of tactile memory. While I have experienced this, it still remains a mystery to me. Sometimes one plays from memory and the mind wanders, thinking of many different things while the fingers continue to play the right notes. Suddenly one's mind returns to the music and wonders how it ever got this far in the piece. Some other compartment of the brain must have told the fingers what to do in the meantime. Singers have often told me that the words help them remember the musical continuity. Most performers say that they play better from memory, and some say they can only perform well when they *don't* look at music.

I envy them all. My memory has played many tricks on me over the years, but its worst feature is that it does not last. If I play a piece several times—the closest I ever come to what is known as practicing—I can retain it briefly, but if I try to play it from memory even a few days later, it has disappeared, except for a snatch here and there. The same applies to my own compositions. I can always reproduce from memory the piece I am working on, but the one that preceded it is no longer there. My memory resembles one of those toy pads given to children: you can write on it, lift the top sheet to erase what you have written, put the sheet back and write something else. It is not a suitable instrument for long-term storage.

Long-term storage was not my problem when my memory failed me during Scriabin's second sonata; I had just learned the piece. Perhaps if I had not made such a final decision so quickly, if I had tried to overcome this weakness, I could have become a concert pianist. Did I use this perhaps deliberate failure as an excuse to do what I was determined to do anyway? Did this miserable event alone convince me that I could trust my ability to improvise but not my ability to remember?

Many performers have problems with memory and have found ways to overcome them. A well-known violinist, one with a large repertory on his memorized list, told me that he once had a memory slip in the opening movement of the Tchaikovsky violin concerto. Now, whenever he plays the piece—and he must do so often every season—and comes to that spot, he remembers his slip. "Have you ever made the same mistake again?" I asked him. "Oh, no," he replied. "I simply remember the fact that I slipped there." Enviable fellow; he *had* conquered his memory by willpower.

Musicians are fond of talking of performances they've

heard and claiming to remember every detail about them, even when many years have passed. "I happened to be present," they will say, "when Toscanini conducted Ravel's 'Bolero.' He took it faster than Ravel had indicated in the score." Or: "Weingartner's *Tristan* overture was slower than anyone else's, but, boy, was it full of intensity!" Can they really remember fifty years later the exact tempo Furt-wängler took in Beethoven's Fifth? Memory, oh, memory!

Some years ago I visited my sister in the kibbutz in which she had spent most of her life. Her husband had died a year earlier, and we were alone together for the first time in many years. One evening we began to compare memories of our childhood.

Did she remember how I had once placed all of her dolls on the Victrola, then wound it up, let it go and watched her dolls fly all over the room?

She did not.

Did I remember that when our assorted uncles came to visit bearing boxes of candy, our mother would lock the candy in a cupboard and hand us one piece each day after dinner?

I did not.

Did she remember that after being told never to eat cucumbers, yoghurt and tea at the same meal, we had de-cided to try the experiment one afternoon and afterward fully expected to get horribly sick or die?

She did not.

With my sister, at a time of which we have such
different memories

Did I remember how suspiciously friendly our mother had become with that well-dressed gentleman with a dark mustache during one of our summer vacations?

I had not noticed him.

Did she remember how I teased her when one of her boyfriends was doing his year of military service, because all our maids also went out with soldiers on Sunday afternoon?

He had not been her boyfriend at all.

Did I remember how she came running home in tears after being told "the facts of life"?

I did not.

Did she remember how our father had removed his service revolver from his desk in order to get rid of it inconspicuously a few days after the Germans came to Vienna? It had made such a strong impression on me.

No, she did not even know that our father had a revolver.

So it went, all afternoon and evening. There were a few memories we *did* share. She remembered my nickname and I hers, but on the whole, brother and sister, only two years apart, raised in the same house by the same parents, had totally different recollections and recognized few of the images the other had retained.

I hope Alexander Nikolayevich Scriabin will forgive me for bringing all this up in his name. As atonement I will play that second sonata of his tonight, but not from memory.

Would it not be a shock if I suddenly *could* play it from memory? I will also play his prelude for the left hand alone, of which I am fond, but I will cheat a little and use both hands.

The musician with the most phenomenal memory I ever encountered was Dimitri Mitropoulos. It was said that he had a photographic memory, and it is true that he could simply look at a score and then rehearse it from memory. The stress here is on the word *rehearse;* many conductors who perform from memory still rehearse with a score. To rehearse without one means that the conductor must detect his musicians' errors, if any, without referring to the score. Mitropoulos could and did do that. He even remembered rehearsal numbers.

Equally astounding to me was Leonard Bernstein's feat of what might be called unintended memorization. The New York Philharmonic gives each concert four times, the first on Thursday evening and the last the following Sunday. When Leonard Bernstein conducted my Concerto for Viola, Strings and Percussion, he stood very straight during the Thursday-night performance, his head in the score. By Saturday he only glanced at it occasionally, and on Sunday not at all. I am sure that he never looked at it between those concerts.

Let me try to describe the kind of memory I need, and that luckily I have, for my essential work, composing. I have to be able to retain the concept of the whole work in my mind while absorbed in its details. This memory has to be flawless, without any holes. It is almost like an obsession, present day and night, which grips the mind until the particular work is completed. Then it is discarded—actually, it discards itself. If I don't make a clean copy of my sketches, after two weeks I sometimes cannot decipher them. I no longer know what they mean—for example, whether that little *o* above the C-sharp meant oboe or a violin harmonic. In other words, I have a short memory, but a very intense one.

On the other hand, the theory that everything is recorded in our memory and needs only to be tapped in order to surface also seems to apply to me. Occasionally I will go to a concert to hear some music I wrote twenty years ago and have not heard since. As I listen, sudden memories are unexpectedly evoked: the moment when I first thought of its main musical idea; the place where it occurred; something said to me about the piece by a person I had not thought of in the twenty intervening years.

In 1982, when I went to Boston to attend rehearsals and the premiere of my violin concerto with Itzhak Perlman and the Boston Symphony, I was interviewed by Robert J. Lurtsema, one of the brightest and most inquisitive radio interviewers. Near the end of the program he said: "Now I will play a short recording, which has been in our library for a great many years. Let us see if you recognize it." Out of the studio speakers came the sound of a piano, recorded monophonically. A strange nostalgia came over me. I knew that the music was by me, I knew that it was by a very young me, but I did not know what it was. Just before it ended, recognition came in a flash. "That was Menahem Pressler, playing a piece of mine called 'Lullaby for Amittai,' " I was able to tell Mr. Lurtsema.

Many years ago, before he joined the Beaux Arts Trio, Menahem Pressler had made a recording of music composed especially for children. His son had been born a short while before, and he had asked me to write a little piece for the album. His son's name was Amittai, rhyming with "lullaby": hence "Lullaby for Amittai." It all came back when I heard those sounds: the hotel room in New York where Menahem told me about the project; the baby boy in a crib during a visit; the smile on his wife's face when I played the piece for them; the picture, drawn by a child, on the record jacket. I took it from Lurtsema's hand to verify my memory; it was all there.

Why, then, the disaster with the Scriabin sonata so many years ago?

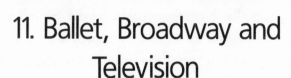

11. Ballet, Broadway and Television

Herbert Ross is now a well-known filmmaker, but when I first met him in 1959 he was a talented young choreographer whose work had begun to draw favorable attention and who had just married Nora Kaye, one of the great dramatic ballerinas. He had formed a new company, called Ballets of Two Worlds, with dancers from Europe and America and headquarters in Belgium. They were to make their debut at the 1960 Berlin Festival, and one of their evenings was to be a new ballet based on the play *The Dybbuk,* with Nora Kaye in the leading part. After hearing a performance of my "Ariel (Visions of Isaiah)," a work for soloists, chorus and orchestra, at a concert in New York, Ross asked me to write the music for his *Dybbuk.*

I had never seen the famous Habimah (Hebrew National Theater) production of S. Ansky's play but had heard about it since my childhood, when it ran for some weeks in Vienna. It is considered a major contribution by Eastern European Jewry to the theater, and since it has Kabbalistic and other mystical elements—the dybbuk is an evil spirit who takes complete possession of afflicted people and can be exorcised only by ritual—the play has had considerable success in Western Europe and the United States. I was deeply interested in all aspects of the story and felt I could create music suitable to its milieu and style.

At that time I had written only two scores for dance: *Masque* for Nina Fonaroff and *Indeterminate Figure* for Daniel Nagrin (which, incidentally, is still in the active repertory of the José Limón Company). The invitation to provide music for an evening-length ballet on a topic so close to my heart excited me, and although there was little time between my first meeting with Ross and the date set for a Berlin premiere, I agreed with enthusiasm to do it. We met several times at the Rosses' apartment in New York, and I listened intently to Herbert's ideas about how he wanted to present the story choreographically. Nora Kaye was always present at these meetings and made many useful comments. If Herbert got carried away by his flow of ideas, she would gently point out difficulties in executing them.

In brief, the plot of *The Dybbuk* centers on Leah's love for Channon, a poor student. Her father, a wealthy man, forces her to marry another suitor. At the wedding the soul of Channon, who has died because of his thwarted love, enters her as a dybbuk, and a rabbi has to be called to exorcise it. He succeeds in doing so, but in the process Leah dies and is thus reunited with her lover in death—in short, an Eastern European *Liebestod*. Herbert had steeped himself in Jewish mysticism and gave me a number of books to read, including a pseudoscientific interpretation which stated that the bride probably had epileptic fits.

Nothing so prosaic entered Herbert's thinking. In his treatment he mixed realism with fantasy and added both people and scenes to the original play. The ballet was to open with Channon's prayer, in which he invokes Kabbalistic forces. He declares his love for Leah by speaking a sentence from the opening chapter of the Song of Songs: "Behold, thou art fair, my love." This sentence becomes important later because when Leah is possessed by the dybbuk, her lover's voice speaks it out of her mouth, but in a distorted fashion. We discussed various ways in which such a distortion could be obtained without losing the comprehensibility of the words.

Electronic music was then fairly new, and we went to the Columbia-Princeton electronic studio and listened to a number of electronic distortions of human speech. Perhaps the equipment was still rather primitive then, but none of the purely electronic solutions seemed satisfactory. Next we met with an actor Herbert knew to hear what he could do with the line. Whatever he did was not enough of a distortion and sounded hysterical in the wrong way. Having played around with tape recorders a little, I then proposed to record the actor reading the line in a deadpan voice, but phonetically backwards. I wrote it out for him: "Vol ym, raif tra outh, dloheb." We recorded it, then played the tape backwards, and it worked amazingly well. It sounded as though the voice had great difficulty in speaking, and wherever the actor inhaled, it came out as a strange exhalation. It was eerie, and few people who heard it ever guessed how we made the line sound that way.

Another scene we discussed was the moment when Leah is first possessed by the dybbuk. She was to walk around and around the chuppah, the wedding canopy, becoming more and more agitated, until suddenly Channon's voice is heard coming out of her. Then she goes wild and has to be restrained by the guests and her father. When I later saw this at a rehearsal I understood why Nora had wanted to dance Leah. She was so frighteningly convincing that I completely lost myself watching her in this scene.

More conventionally balletic were to be such sequences as Leah's dancing with the beggars in the second act. I decided to use a small instrumental combination of violin, clarinet, bass and drum to accompany this, the sort of typical klezmer combination one might find at an Eastern European party. I also looked forward to writing the music for the exorcism, and of course for the "love-death." Just before the exorcism Herbert was planning to have a procession of penitents, Jewish flagellanti, cross the stage. We decided that they would not only move and dance but repeatedly intone a Hebrew sentence: "Ashamnu, ashamnu, chatanu mikol am" (We have sinned, we have sinned more than any other people). I used the rhythm of those words in the percussion section of the orchestra as the exorcism approached its climax.

The third act was to begin with a lullaby, which a nurse was to sing to the ailing Leah. At first I looked through books of Jewish folk songs to find a good melody; then I remembered what Darius Milhaud had said to me that summer at Tanglewood: "Always write your own folk songs." I decided to follow his advice and wrote a wordless lullaby, a simple diatonic, slightly modal tune; after all, no child would fall asleep to a twelve-tone row. It was sung by a lovely mezzo-soprano, and I later developed the melody in the orchestra in a scene called "Leah's Dream." Writing that lullaby convinced me that in music for the theater all theoretical or abstract considerations have no value; only human gestures and needs matter.

After Herbert and I had agreed on most major questions he gave me a typed outline of the sequence and succession of dances, with the projected duration for each of them; then he left for Europe to start training and rehearsing his new company. I did not perceive this outline as a diminution of my worth or a restriction on my freedom. I remembered seeing the instructions Tchaikovsky had been given when he was asked to write the *Nutcracker,* including the exact number of bars for each dance.

Since I had so little time, I took a leave of absence from Juilliard and shut myself up in a cabin at the MacDowell Colony in New Hampshire, where I have since taken refuge a number of times when I had a deadline and needed to get away from the telephone and other distractions. First I did a piano score and sent it, section by section, as I completed it, to Berlin, where it went into rehearsal as soon as it arrived. In the evenings I scored what I had written during the day, and then sent the orchestral score to Brussels, where the instrumental parts were to be copied. The overseas telephone did not yet function the way it does today, and I was quite on my own with Herbert's script and my recollection of our discussions.

I finished the music in time and flew to Berlin, full of hope and excitement, to be present at final rehearsals and the premiere. When I arrived I found Herbert, Nora and their entire company in deep gloom. The impresario of the company had not been financially sound, to put it mildly. The set was cheaply built and kept falling apart, as did the ill-fitting costumes of the dancers. They had not been given proper ballet slippers either. The musicians must have been recruited from the beer gardens of Berlin, for few of them could play the notes properly. No one in the company had been paid in two weeks. The night before the premiere, the impresario disappeared—he was never heard from again— but the company decided to go through with the opening anyway and prepare for the worst. The premiere was indeed almost a disaster—so much went wrong that it still pains me to think of it—and led to the collapse of the company. It was a pity because, if nothing else, Nora Kaye's dancing

At the MacDowell Colony in 1966
CLEMENS KALISHER

was so powerful that it left me breathless every time I saw it. The night we knew that it was all over, we went to the only Chinese restaurant in Berlin, and as we sat down Nora said with a wistful sigh, "Now I can eat."

I believe this was the last time Nora Kaye danced in public. For me the consequences were less tragic; eventually I made a suite out of the *Dybbuk* music, and it has been played by a number of orchestras. For Herbert the consequences of our Berlin disaster were decisive, but in a different way. He must have sworn to himself never to be in such a situation again, and turned his attention to Broadway. He had not yet been asked to direct a show, but he did choreograph the dances for a big new musical then going into rehearsal. The show was called *The Gay Life,* at a time— not so long ago—when the word "gay" meant carefree and happy. Set in Vienna, it was based on a Schnitzler story, and the score was by Arthur Schwartz, one of the most melodious Broadway composers.

Perhaps because he thought he owed me something (I had never received the second half of my *Dybbuk* commission), perhaps because the show was set in Vienna and the two main dance sequences were to be a czardas and a waltz, Herbert asked me to do the dance music for *The Gay Life.* I had never seen a Broadway production from backstage and my curiosity was aroused.

I took yet another leave of absence from Juilliard and began rehearsals with Herbert and some sixteen dancers in an empty theater on the Lower East Side of Manhattan. (By a curious coincidence, it was a theater that had been used for Yiddish plays and must have had its share of dybbuks.) Though we tried to turn Arthur Schwartz's tunes into a czardas and a waltz, we soon discovered that while they were lovely melodies, they did not lend themselves to that, and I was given permission to do my own. Careful readers of Broadway programs will know that therein lies the difference between "dance arrangements" and "dance music."

My contract with the producers of *The Gay Life* called for several hours of rehearsal every day, and I fully expected to play the piano for long hours. What I did not foresee was that much of the dance and the music that was created was improvised at these rehearsals. It was a new way of working for me. I had always loved to improvise but not in public, and it took me a while to get used to this way of working. But it also was my first opportunity to watch dances being created. I watched Herbert using the bodies of his dancers similarly to how I use the keys of my piano; I saw him incorporate occasional spontaneous movements that they made into the dance itself, just as my fingers sometimes seem to create music on their own. In effect, he was improvising with the bodies of others. I also observed him training an actress who had done little singing or dancing to make spectacular moves in her czardas.

During the rehearsals I got to know some of the dancers,

and to my surprise they were all solid, friendly, helpful people, by no means the women of easy morals that has been the stereotype of chorus girls. Rehearsals were long but rarely tedious, and after a section was set, a proper rehearsal pianist took over to play the endless repetitions necessary for technical and light rehearsals and run-throughs for various purposes.

As soon as all the dances were set, our rehearsals were moved uptown and the dances were incorporated into the action of the play. I began to realize that the ideas of many people contribute to a Broadway show, and that unless there is a strong director to unify these varied ideas, they do not always form a coherent whole. For the music alone there were four people: the composer of the songs, the composer of the dance music, the writer of the "continuity" (introductions and transitions) and the orchestrator, all of them skilled in their own fields but not necessarily alike in taste and style.

As the show went into full rehearsal, a great many people came to watch and make comments. Some of them must have been backers, because they were listened to even when what they proposed made little sense. One particularly unpleasant character, an older man, always sucking with moist lips on a half-burned cigar, always with a different, cheap-looking blonde at his side, made truly asinine suggestions. None of them were incorporated into the show, but they were all tried, at considerable loss of expensive time.

When the musical went to the Fisher Theater in Detroit for tryouts, things got even worse. I watched in mounting horror as it underwent innumerable changes, few of them for the better. Some of the original jokes were really funny, but when the Detroit audience did not laugh long or loudly enough, they were replaced by silly slapstick ones. A few days before my contract expired, the man with the cigar reappeared and proposed that the show open with a ballet. Both Herbert and I knew that this was wrong, but we had to oblige. The opening ballet was thrown out the next week.

The waste was appalling. There was a lovely set by Oliver Smith of a bridge over an imagined river, and Anita Gillette sang a song while standing on it; as I recall, she was contemplating suicide. At some point, for reasons I never learned, it was decided not to use the song. Out with the song went the bridge, the whole scene and its set. I asked the production stage manager what would happen to the set —I had been told that it had cost fifteen thousand dollars to build, at a time when an entire off-Broadway production had a budget of seven to eight thousand dollars—and he said that it would be destroyed. In my naïveté I asked whether it couldn't be used by some other show, and was laughed at.

Those weeks in Detroit were not easy for me. All my life I had gotten up early and done my important work before noon. Here rehearsals never began before eleven, lasted most of the day and were followed by an evening performance, with meetings, discussions or parties afterward. Many of the actors and dancers needed a couple of hours to unwind, whereas I had trouble staying awake. All day long new changes would be practiced during rehearsals, but the evening performance was generally the old version. Just to keep the two separate in one's mind was difficult.

We stayed in one of those downtown residential hotels within walking distance of the theater and the railroad station that must have been built for actors at a time when all travel was by train. Each room had cooking facilities, though not a separate kitchen; there were all kinds of beds —folding, pull-out and ones that came off the wall. I kept a bottle of whisky in my room, and every day, after the maid had cleaned, the level of the fluid was down about half an inch. I did not really mind, but one day, when I entered the room and found her there, I offered her a drink. She blushed and declined, and after that the fluid level remained the same. My colleagues told me that she was simply replenishing the bottle with water.

The producers of *The Gay Life* must have realized that their show was in trouble because they hired a new director, a so-called play doctor. I do not know how he saved the ailing patient—my contract expired soon after he was engaged—but when the show opened in New York a few weeks later, it was a success and ran for several months. My dance music received good notices, and soon I had offers from other Broadway producers and choreographers. I chose to return to my studio, to improvise alone behind closed doors and to write music under conditions that allowed me to be in control of the final result.

For Herbert Ross the show was an important event, the beginning of a transition from choreography to directing, and eventually to films. His first great success, *The Turning Point,* dealt with the ballet world, and I like to think that Nora Kaye sat in the background and gave advice as he directed.

The only other time in my life I came near what might be called the commercial world was when I wrote music for documentary films. Some years ago CBS Television had a documentary program late on Sunday afternoon called *Twentieth Century* that dealt with significant events that had taken place in our era, many of them wars. Walter Cronkite was the narrator, and CBS asked a number of serious composers to provide the music. To my regret I never met Cronkite because, although his voice and my music were often heard together, they were recorded at separate sessions.

In writing for film or television the composer has nothing to do with the shaping of the artistic entity and he is called in only when filming is completed. He then watches the film with the producer and director, who tell him where music will be needed or would be most suitable. They do not always tell him where there will be sound effects that may drown out his music, or where there will be narration, which must always be audible. Then the composer times the sections he is to underscore and jots down where transitions take place.

The recording sessions for these programs are of the highest professional level. The orchestra is made up of the best free-lance musicians in New York, men and women who can read anything at sight, and never play it that well again because the second time around they are already bored. This is a slight exaggeration, but these studio musicians, including those on the West Coast, are really a unique breed. The conductor for the *Twentieth Century* series was the late Alfredo Antonini, also a top professional for this kind of work. He did not record while watching the film, as some others do, but his sense of time and timing was quite uncanny. If the change from somber sounds to sprightly ones was supposed to come after two minutes and forty-seven seconds, Antonini was always on the dot. We never had to rerecord because he was early or late.

I had once been told that film music is good only when it is not noticed. Whether this is true or not, I felt highly flattered when CBS decided not to have *any* sound effects during a naval battle, so that viewers could listen to my battle music undisturbed by cannon shots.

Writing for that prestigious series led to invitations to write for others. I remember one producer saying to me as he gave me directions, "As far as style is concerned, you can write whatever you want—just not any of that twelve-tone stuff." Some nasty quirk in me impelled me to write one little sequence for the film in strict twelve-tone. It turned out to be the section the producer liked best, but I never told him.

Many people lament the fact that there is so little good music on television. It may not be wise to say so, but pure music—absolute music—was never intended for and is in essence not suitable for visual presentation. Music can be listened to with one's eyes closed. Perhaps the highest degree of concentration is reached, as it is in meditation, with eyes closed, shutting out everything but the sound, its significance and meaning. What does television do? It shows us the fingers of the pianist going up and down the keyboard, the gaping mouth of the tenor, the contortions on the face of the conductor. Television directors know their scores well, or they have someone sit next to them who does. When the flute plays, we are shown the flutist's quivering lips; when the timpanist lowers his sticks, we see them hit the drum; when the cellist has an expressive passage, we see his vibrating finger on the string or the deepening furrows on his forehead. Directors almost never make obvious mistakes like showing the trumpet while the oboe is playing. Yet all these pictures are distractions that keep us from concentrating on the essence of the music. To be sure, when we sit in a concert hall we look at the performers, but our

eyes are not commanded to do so in accordance with someone else's tempo and taste. Some people *do* have visual
reactions to music, or even pictorial ones. Whether you
liked it or not, Walt Disney's *Fantasia* was a genuine attempt to convey those reactions artistically. Everyone has
his own little fantasias when listening to music, but there
can never be a universal visual reaction to music.

Music in conjunction with theater or dance, on the other
hand, is eminently suitable for television. Since religious
institutions of all denominations have always been among
the most intelligent users of music, it is perhaps not a
coincidence that some of the best original programs done
on television have been presented under the umbrella of
religion. I am referring to the two Sunday-morning series
that Pamela Ilott produced for CBS, to which many prominent writers, poets, composers, directors and choreographers
contributed new works, vaguely related to biblical themes
but quite unrestricted otherwise. I see no similar efforts on
public television these days.

Admittedly these programs ran at an hour when most
people were sleeping off their Saturday night hangovers.
Their viewing audience was small by television standards,
but still large in the eyes of the serious artist. There were
no commercial interruptions—what advertiser would be
foolish enough to try to sell his product on a Sunday
morning?—and thus it was possible to build dramatically

and aim for a unity of vision. These programs went on for many years, and I was involved on several occasions. I did "The Story of Esther" with Anna Sokolow and several programs with John Butler. Of all the choreographers I worked with, I think Butler best understood the strengths and weaknesses of the medium; he used close-ups showing details of movement and expression rather than magnificent tableaus in which the individual dancer became so small as to be almost invisible.

Since the budget for these programs was small, they rarely had a full orchestra, but when dealing with recorded sound, a few wisely chosen instruments can create almost any effect. I used only four instrumentalists and four percussionists in my *Images of Man,* a work commissioned by CBS for presentation at the National Cathedral in Washington in 1973. The text came from *The Four Zoas* by William Blake; hence everything was in fours, except for the meter. The television camera roamed over the inside of that magnificent church, ascended to the stained-glass windows and settled on the intent faces of the choirboys, who sang my music with pure young voices. Another program without dance that I wrote for that series was "The Story of Joseph," with Roberta Peters singing and Hal Linden as a very effective narrator. Pamela Ilott also sent her crew to film *The Last Lover,* my chamber opera with libretto by Gail Godwin, at its Caramoor premiere.

My contribution to Broadway was both small and brief —and without Herbert Ross it might not have happened at all. I wish that today there was more original musical theater on television, rather than the standard operatic fare. Better still, there should be time and interest for both.

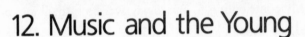

12. Music and the Young

SHOULD a musician teach his own children? Leopold Mozart would have emphatically said yes; so would most of the Bachs, including Johann Sebastian. But many people today don't think it a good idea, and I listened to them. Their argument runs that too much intimacy causes problems, and that strangers surmount these better. I have only one child and I did not teach him music. He did not become a musician; it was never even considered. This was not a disappointment to me, since I firmly believe that only people to whom making music means more than anything else in the world should become professional musicians, and that they usually prevail, whatever the barriers placed in their way. I once had a student whose parents forced him to study medicine. He obeyed and got his M.D., but today he is conducting the orchestra of a touring ballet company.

My son, Dan, did show an early interest in music. Not only did his small fingers press down keys on the piano; they also took up a pencil and drew large notes on music paper, some with noses, eyes and ears, others more like the moon and stars. His particular joy was doing this on onionskin

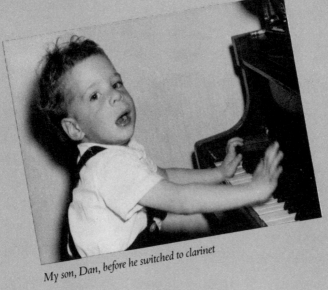

My son, Dan, before he switched to clarinet

paper, which we then took together to the blueprinters and watched how black-and-white copies of his drawings and my music came out the other end of the ozalid machine.

Dan's first piano teacher was one of my Juilliard students. At that time I thought youthful enthusiasm was more important than patience and experience. Unfortunately, this young teacher, intent on impressing me, made extraordinary demands upon Dan, the kind perhaps only a young Mozart could have fulfilled. He was also too rigid about the proper position of the hand in playing. Dan did not progress well, and my wife and I decided to stop the lessons before he turned against music altogether. Since he was an only child and destined to remain one, the piano seemed too solitary an activity for one who was alone so much of the time. We felt that he should switch to an instrument that would allow him to join others in making music. Dan liked the idea and proposed the trumpet. To share the apartment with a kid practicing the trumpet seemed a sacrifice even the most loving parents should not have to make, so after some haggling we settled on the clarinet, an instrument with a fine repertoire, both in solo and in chamber music, and also suitable for playing in a band or orchestra. We found an excellent, experienced teacher with whom Dan worked for many years.

When he became older, Dan insisted on having a set of drums so that he could join a rock group. Since then I have consoled many parents who become desperate when their sons reach this age; I tell them that the phase will pass, usually after a year. It *does* pass, but that year is a loud one. When Dan was not actually bashing his drums or rehearsing with his group in our house, he listened to the radio. I briefly became an expert on the rock music of the period. I was teaching at both Juilliard and Brooklyn College then, and when I mentioned Jefferson Airplane or The Grateful Dead to my Juilliard students, they did not know what I was talking about. My Brooklyn College students knew only too well; they were also impressed by my knowing.

Dan had one very intense summer of classical music at a well-run summer camp when he was in his late teens, and he sang in a glee club during his college years. He took no music courses while in college, not even Music Appreciation, which would have given him an easy *A*. Since then his need for active music-making has occasionally surfaced. While traveling around the world after having finished college, he asked that his clarinet be sent to him in India, where he was spending some time in a monastery. Later, while climbing in Nepal, he was the guest of a mountain tribe for some weeks. One evening, after they had sung for him they asked him to reciprocate. The only piece that came to his mind, he said, was an excerpt from a choral work of mine. He sang it and they liked it; this Nepalese mountain is probably the most remote place my music has ever been heard. Today Dan is an intelligent, informed listener who gets great pleasure out of music.

Though I did not teach my own son, I have taught a great many sons and daughters of other people over the years—not children, since my early days in Jerusalem, but young adults at professional schools and at a liberal arts college. This is not meant to diminish the importance of early training, for childhood is when the foundation for musical understanding is laid. To teach small children, however, is a special gift that I do not think I possess.

When one teaches harmony, counterpoint or musical literature at a school like Juilliard, many young people pass through one's classes who later become prominent performers. One can usually predict their future even then, although not all who show precocious talent mature into great artists. The brightest, most anxious-to-learn young singer to come to Sergius Kagen's and my vocal literature classes was Leontyne Price. She also had a warm, outgoing personality, great interpretative facility and a singularly beautiful voice. There was never a doubt in anyone's mind that she would go far. Jan de Gaetani and Bethany Beardslee also took the same class. They were both intelligent students who have done well with their natural endowment.

Sometimes we were given advance warning when an exceptional student was about to arrive. When Pinchas Zukerman came to Juilliard, Isaac Stern called me to say that an extraordinarily talented young violinist had arrived from Israel, and would I please give him my attention. Pinky, as we called him, entered my third-year Literature and Materi-

als of Music class and was a most delightful student, full of
ideas, wit and humor. At the end of the school year, the class
was working on orchestration. The final assignment for each
student was to orchestrate a page or two of piano music of
their own choice. Pinky came to see me and pleaded for an
exemption; he was going to play with Pablo Casals at the
festival in Puerto Rico and also was just about to be married. I felt I should be strict and told him that he could not
get a passing grade unless he turned in his final paper. I
wonder what would have happened if I had "flunked"
Pinchas Zukerman. A colleague of mine once threatened
Van Cliburn with this fate and was promptly called into the
dean's office and asked to desist. Luckily I was not put into
this quandary; the day before I had to turn in my grades a
package arrived from Puerto Rico, special delivery, regis-
tered, express mail: it was Pinky's orchestration.

The grand old lady of the piano at Juilliard was Rosina
Lhévinne. She taught until her mid-nineties and at her
ninetieth birthday party looked no older than fifty. Occasionally she sent me private students for specific reasons. Her
voice on the telephone, heavy with a Russian accent and
omitting all unnecessary words, would sound something
like this: "Have student from Argentina. Plenty money.
Good fingers, not much upstairs. You teach her *music.*"

Once she called me to discuss a fourteen-year-old boy
who was flying in from Cincinnati every other week for a
piano lesson with her. She thought the boy phenomenally

talented—those were the words she used—and asked me to teach him the theoretical subjects in private lessons so that he could enter Juilliard, but would not have to sit in theory classes for four years. She also thought the boy might not remain a pianist, but would perhaps become a conductor. I worked with him for a while—"phenomenally talented" was no exaggeration—and he did indeed pass his Juilliard qualifying exams in theory. His name is James Levine and he is now director of the Metropolitan Opera in New York.

Ear-training was part of the Literature and Materials of Music curriculum during the late sixties at Juilliard. It was arranged so that if I taught the usage of a certain chord in one class, a teaching fellow would have the students practice hearing it during the succeeding hour. (I have never taught ear-training myself; having absolute pitch, I do not know how to help students who have trouble hearing.) While observing ear-training sessions I came to the conclusion that too much time is spent on solfège and other systems of melodic hearing, and not enough on rhythm. Yet inability to grasp rhythmic patterns quickly and precisely is the most serious cause of poor sight-reading, and poor sight-reading is a severe handicap for the developing musician. The only book that deals with the problem is Hindemith's *Elementary Training for Musicians,* an excellent book with one decisive drawback: it jumps too quickly from the simple to the complex. One day, while at my publisher's office, I discussed this with Lewis Roth, my editor at the time. I said, "Someone ought to do a book that teaches rhythm slowly, systematically and progressively." He answered quickly, "Why don't you?"

Later that year I was on jury duty. It was August, stiflingly hot, and all the judges must have been on vacation. We sat in that dreary waiting room of the State Supreme Court for two weeks, and very few people were called. Most men—women were still exempt from jury duty then —slept, played cards or memorized the newspaper. I decided to use my time better; I brought music paper with me every morning and began to invent the one hundred exercises that make up my book *Rhythmic Training*. (Later I considered dedicating the book to the criminal-court system of New York.)

By the time my book appeared in print, Juilliard had separated ear-training from other theoretical subjects, so I never had a chance to try my system in class. It has since been adopted by many professional schools and colleges, has been translated into Japanese and has made me friends and enemies. Jazz musicians often write to say that the book has helped them. Recently I received a postcard that read: "Dear Mr. Starer: I who worship the genius of Art Tatum (he's very much alive though gone) do hereby express my appreciation and gratitude for your *Rhythmic Training*."

Not everyone does. A few summers ago Gail and I took a leisurely trip through the Blue Ridge Mountains. When we came to a lovely summer resort called Blowing Rock, in North Carolina, she remembered a restaurant there in which all the waiters were voice students at various music schools who were earning money during their vacations. Of course we went there for dinner. The restaurant was at the edge of a mountain and had a superb view. Between serving meals to their customers, waiters stood on a small stage in the center and sang solos and duets for us. When conversation with our waiter revealed that I taught at Juilliard, he asked my name. "Oh," he said, "you're *that* man." Within minutes four of the waiters appeared onstage and put on a skit performing some of the exercises in my book. Apparently they always had a copy to practice with when business was slow. At the end one of the four waiters who had been in the skit, a pretty young girl, came to our table and said half in earnest, half in flirtation, and in an accent I could not imitate if I lived a hundred years, "At Converse College they made us use your book. Lord, how I hated you!"

In the fall of 1985 I was on jury duty again, this time in civil court. When you give your profession as "musician" or "professor," most lawyers will reject you as unsuitable for jury duty. "Musician" must conjure up an image of a seedy individual playing a piano late at night in a bar, a cigarette dangling from his mouth; "professor" probably suggests a hair-splitting pedant who will never reach a conclusion since he always sees both sides to an argument. Whatever the lawyers' reasons, it meant another two weeks in a waiting room. Seventeen years had elapsed since the publication of *Rhythmic Training,* and I thought it was time to do a simpler version of it for the young and the adult beginner. It is called *Basic Rhythmic Training.* I hope the state of New York will forgive me for having thus spent my time.

Teaching harmony, counterpoint and similar subjects at a liberal arts college is in some ways more rewarding than doing so at a professional school. When given an assignment in theory, the typical Juilliard student does it reluctantly and often with the attitude that "I should really be practicing my instrument." To the college student, on the other hand, theory is the core of his work and he gives it his complete attention. Also, colleges allow the teacher to pursue his own interests more. When a topic interests me, I propose a graduate course in it and thus get a chance to look into a subject of my choice in the company of, and with the help of, ten to twelve young intelligent minds. Topics I have pursued in recent years include: "The Lied from Mozart to Mahler," "The Fugue since Bach" and "Variations, Form and Technique." My next one will be a comparison of early and late music by composers who lived more than fifty years.

I have not done much teaching of composition. People often ask whether musical composition can really be taught. Only up to a point, I reply, or as much as writing and painting can be taught. Certain techniques can be acquired, such as orchestration; certain devices must be mastered, such as invertible counterpoint; but the application of these and similar skills differs with each individual.

There are two kinds of students of composition: those who look to the outside, and those who look inside themselves. Those who look to the outside are relatively easy to teach: one makes them study scores by living composers and sends them to concerts of modern music. Before long they will write their "Ligeti piece," their "Crumb piece" and their "Glass piece." Stylistic imitation is not difficult, and these students will eventually be teaching it in their own courses of composition.

The other kind, the ones who look inside themselves, are much more difficult to deal with. There is little one can do for them concretely except listen to their problems (which are not always musical), encourage them constantly (even criticism mustn't discourage) and advise them whenever possible. If they have talent, stamina and persistence they will become composers.

I have not taught children in many years, but I have written music for them all my life. During the year that Dan took piano lessons I wrote a set of pieces called *Sketches in Color*. While looking for sounds to match colors, I observed Dan in order to discover what children like and dislike. Children do not like bombast or boredom, and they see through pretentiousness much better than adults do. When I took nine-year-old Dan to the Venice Biennale he stopped in front of a painting by one of our most famous contemporary artists, a painting that had a roll of toilet paper stuck in it. After looking at it for a while, he turned around and asked, "Did a grown-up really do this?"

Children should make music, not just have to endure it passively. The child who has made music will always have a better understanding of it and gain greater pleasure from it later in life than the child who has never played it. No early lessons are a total waste, even if they are discontinued before the child has reached any degree of proficiency on an instrument.

All the great composers of the past have written music for children, none of it with condescension and much of it of interest to adults. Their music for children is always clear and relatively simple, two qualities acceptable to all ages. Much of it is written for the piano, the instrument most children were taught before the twentieth century. Today children play every instrument, and there is great need for original music for orchestra, band and chorus. The young should not only be exposed to simplified arrangements of masterpieces, but should become acquainted with the music of their time. The limitations to be considered when writing for the young are not overly restrictive: hands are small, endurance is more limited, grasp of complexities is less developed.

Publishers clamor for music suitable for young players,

and some schools even commission pieces for themselves. These commissions can be quite specific in their requirements. Some years ago the Dalton Schools in New York asked me to write a piece for their orchestra. The stipulation was that it could be played with any number of flutes and clarinets, but without oboes and bassoons; that it use many trumpets but few horns; that it employ as many percussion players as possible; and that it have not only first and second violins, but also third violins, who would play only open strings. The combination must have been more practical than I thought, because *Dalton Set,* the piece I wrote for them, has been picked up not only by many other schools but also by adult amateur orchestras. Just the other day the mail brought a program in which a doctors' orchestra had played *Dalton Set* in the second-floor hall of their hospital.

Even more demanding was a more recent commission from the Third Street Settlement Music School. I was told that their preschool division was very capable on Orff instruments, and that I should try to incorporate them in the orchestra. I had only a vague knowledge of Orff instruments and went to the school to look them over. I found them to be an assortment of xylophone-type instruments tuned in the pentatonic scale, the five-note scale usually associated with Far Eastern music. Since I normally use all twelve notes, this was a challenge, but after giving the request considerable thought, I found a way of working these instruments into my music without sacrificing my own style and individuality. When *Third Street Overture* had its festive premiere at Alice Tully Hall, seven little girls in very pretty dresses sat in front of the conventional orchestra, mallets in their hands, and at a dramatically selected spot began banging away on their miniature xylophones, adding percussive joy to the fabric of sound. I was amused to read in next morning's newspaper that I had written an "ethnic" piece. The reviewer had concluded that since the Third Street Music School was in New York's Lower East Side, near Chinatown, I had used the pentatonic scale to pay homage to this community.

Being with the young keeps us young and, as we all know, the child in us is the creator. We must keep this child alive and let no one restrain it, imprison it or eradicate it. But as the child in us knows, coming to the end of anything—of a piece of music, a voyage, any pleasurable hour—is like a little death. Perhaps we have so many little deaths to prepare us for the big one, the final one.

In music the closing section of a composition is called the coda, which originally meant "tail." Mozart and Prokofiev, among others, had no difficulty with their closing sections. The rock generation does not know they exist, because rock songs never have real endings; they simply fade away. The greatest master of the coda was Beethoven. His take unexpected turns, often bringing back the main ideas of a piece, not to recapitulate, but to show them in a new light, to develop them in a new way, to give us new insights into old experiences.

I want to take a look at the countries and societies I have known and been part of, not merely visited. Nations go through stages just as human beings do; in essence there are only three such stages (not counting birth and death), the first being ascent and the vigor of youth; the second maturity and the height of power; the third decline and the diminishing of vital forces. If you are willing to accept these assumptions perhaps you will bear with me while I take a quick look at countries and societies in terms of where they stood in this scheme when I knew them.

The Austria of my childhood was already past the third stage. Vienna, which had been the proud capital of a multilingual empire, was a disproportionately large city in a small, powerless country whose citizens were divided and not altogether unwilling to be absorbed by their mighty northern neighbor.

The Jewish Palestine I knew in my teens had just begun its youthful ascent and was the most idealistic society I have ever known. Today, not even half a century later, the citizens of Israel have proven to the world that Jews can fight. This was necessary after the Holocaust, but in the process they seem to have lost the ability to convince others of the justice of their cause. Stranger still, they seem less able to manage money than their ancestors were.

The British were just beyond their highest peak when I proudly wore their uniform. They fought valiantly, but while they did win the war, it cost them dearly. I still think the English are the most civilized people of Europe; the word "fairness" does not exist in the German or French language. In the fifties and sixties, as one colony after another gained independence, it became no longer true that "the sun never sets on the British Empire."

The United States that I came to as a student in 1947, the country in which I eventually chose to live, the land of my fourth and final nationality—I do not count the German, because it was involuntary—was young, pure and strong when I arrived. It had beaten evil and felt itself untainted by it. An unjust and unjustified war in the sixties drove its youth into opposition, and this seems to me the first sign of the beginning of its decline.

Why all these observations? In order to write a Beethovenesque coda? Perhaps, but mainly to see my own life in relation to that of societies I have been part of. It appears that I have swum against the stream; that I have moved from an old, decaying civilization to a young, powerful one, having touched others in between.

How has all this affected me and my music? I have probably selected what suited me from all the cultures that have touched me, and rejected or ignored what was incompatible with my nature. In my music, I have been told, there are elements of Viennese sentiment, Jewish melisma, Near

Eastern playfulness and American jazz. These elements must have been compatible with my nature to have become part of my style and musical personality. Other features of the cultures I have known did not become part of me. This has led me to believe that while our lives are shaped by events that others control, we do have the choice of accepting from the worlds around us only what can coexist with our essential self.

About the Author

One of the foremost composers working in America today, ROBERT STARER was born in Vienna in 1924. He studied at the State Academy in Vienna, the Jerusalem Conservatory and the Juilliard School, where he taught for many years after his graduation in 1949. Today he is Distinguished Professor of Music at Brooklyn College and the Graduate Center of the City University of New York. Among his honors are two Guggenheim Fellowships and an award from the American Academy and Institute of Arts and Letters. His stage works include ballets for Martha Graham and three operas, two with libretti by Gail Godwin. His symphonic works have been performed by major orchestras here and abroad, with such conductors as Mitropoulos, Steinberg, Bernstein and Mehta.